THE
SECRETS
OF
SPANISH
TENNIS

Second Edition

THE SECRETS OF SPANISH TENNIS

Second Edition

BY CHRIS LEWIT

New Chapter Press

The Secrets to Spanish Tennis is published by New Chapter Press (www.NewChapterMedia.com) and distributed by the IPG (www.IPGBook.com).

ISBN: 978-19375-59984

Front cover photo of Rafael Nadal courtesy of Carine06 via WikiCommons and front cover of Carlos Alcaraz courtesy of J.Crechet3 via WikiComons, Lluis Bruguera photos courtesy of Lluis Bruguera, Emilio Sanchez photo courtesy of Barcex via WikiCommons, Alex Corretja photo courtesy of Maartmeester via WikiCommons, Andres Gimeno courtesy of Dutch National Archives via WikiCommons, Manuel Orantes courtesy of WikiCommons, Manolo Santana photo by Paco Mari via WikiCommons, Arantxa Sanchez Vicario photo by Bill Mitchell via WikiCommons, Sergi Bruguera photos by Sergio Carmona, Garbine Muguruza and Carlos Alcaraz photo courtesy of si.robi via WikiCommons, Carlos Moya photo courtesy of James Barrett via WikiCommons, Juan Carlos Ferrero photo courtesy of Sergio Rulz via WikiCommons, Rafael Nadal photo courtesy of Pahcal123 via WikiCommons, Andy Murray photo courtesy of Yann Caradec via WikiCommons, Albert Costa photo courtesy of WikiCommons, Rafael Nadal photo on page 129 courtesy of Charlie Cowins via WikiCommons

TABLE OF CONTENTS

"This book is dedicated to my amazing wife Kim and my four superstar kids: Sky, Isaiah, Ruby, and Ocean. They all love Spain—but not tennis—just as much as I do!"
—C.L. 2024

ACKNOWLEDGEMENTS

After nearly 20 years of interviews, research and writing, I'm thrilled to offer this updated book to the world community of coaches, parents, and players who are interested in the Spanish style of tennis training. I would like to thank the myriad coaches in Spain who allowed me to interview them and were more than generous with their time.

Specifically, I would like to thank Lluis Bruguera, who has dedicated countless hours of interviews and court time to me, detailing his philosophy and training methods. Lluis has been an incredible resource and mentor to me over many years— and continues to be today—and has allowed me unparalleled access to him both on the court to observe his coaching first-hand and in interviews. Words cannot express the sadness for me that the Bruguera Top Team Academy recently closed following the pandemic. The academy held many memories for me and was one of my favorite clubs to visit in Barcelona. I will miss my study trips to the village of Santa Coloma de Cervello, in the hills of Barcelona, where Bruguera built so many great champions!

I am also extremely grateful to *el guru del tenis,* William Pato Alvarez—may he rest in peace—who not only answered every question I could ask him, but also allowed me to sit on his court to observe his lessons which was a wonderful learning experience. Pato also sold me his autobiography and writings for twenty euros—the best deal I have probably ever made in Spain! I had the works translated and to this day I believe I have the only English translations available. The tennis world lost a great personality and coach with Pato's passing.

Pato's proteges, Emilio Sánchez and Sergio Casal, were also wonderful to learn from in Spain, and Emilio has been an ongoing mentor to me for many years, and continues to be so to this day.

I am also grateful to Toni Nadal, a titan of Spanish tennis, for letting me observe his coaching on courts and for taking the time to let me interview him at the Rafa Nadal Tennis Academy by Movistar in Mallorca. Toni's tactical brilliance and character building principles are unparalleled.

Also, I have a great appreciation for Jofre Porta, who has shared his wisdom selflessly at his academy, Global Tennis, also in Mallorca. He and his wife Afiza always welcome me graciously to their academy just outside of Palma. Jofre has an inquisitive mind, a creative spirit, and he loves to educate and share his knowledge.

In addition, Antonio Cascales, a less well known but not less accomplished coach, was also generous to me with his time in an interview at the Ferrero Tennis Academy in Villena. Antonio is a scholar and educator, and he opened my eyes to the history of Spanish tennis coaching, the relationship between Lluis and Pato, and the influence that the dictator Franco's policies had on the growth and trajectory of tennis in Spain. Cascales has synthesized philosophical coaching elements from across Spain into a cohesive and powerful teaching method that has helped produce two world No. 1 players for Spain, Juan Carlos Ferrero and Carlos Alcaraz.

Miguel Crespo, PhD, offered many valuable insights into the cofactors of success in Spain and also assisted with his sharp editing eye.

Thank you to all the other coaches and important figures who shared insights with me—too many to name—and the elite academies profiled in this book, and to their directors and staff, who opened up their academy operations to me and allowed me to observe and ask many, many questions!

In general, most Spanish coaches are keen to share their knowledge and experience, and to share their understanding of a system that has propelled their country to the pinnacle of international tennis. That being said, as of 2024, the competitive landscape in Spain has dramatically changed, with many new academies cropping up and competing fiercely with each other. Because of this competition, some academies are more guarded and secretive than when I first started traveling to Spain in the early 2000s.

It's also interesting to note that while individual coaches in Spain are very knowledgeable about the method they teach, they often are not familiar with the methods of other clubs and academies around the country. Surprisingly, many Spanish coaches whom I met would ask me what was happening at other academies, even ones geographically close by! They were simply dialed into their own training methods and didn't have a great understanding of other methods being used across the country. By traveling to many different academies and learning multiple approaches, I was able to bridge those knowledge gaps, make novel comparisons and contrasts, and to synthesize disparate coaching styles and systems into broader common themes.

In many ways, the results of the Spanish method have exceeded even the greatest dreams of the early originators and visionaries like Lluis Bruguera and William Pato Álvarez. The continued success of the indefatigable Rafael Nadal and the rise of the charismatic prodigy Carlos Alcaraz have merely capstoned a method and tennis revolution that have already achieved legendary greatness.

FOREWORD – Lluis Bruguera

Many years ago I met Chris and I loved his insatiable curiosity to know the real advantages of the Spanish system that has had so much success over the recent years.

Lluis Bruguera

He has made an excellent work observing the Spanish system and has demonstrated his big capacity of analysis and his big interest and motivation by getting to know many of the leading coaches and academies in Spain.

Chris is in love with the Spanish system and a fervent follower because he believes in the advantages of what this system offers. It's obvious that one country so small and without many practitioners must have something hidden that supports the success.

Chris is an unusual character in the world of education and coaches due to his insatiable curiosity. He is always looking for the why of everything. He has personality and commitment, and he knows how to transmit his knowledge of the Spanish system to help his students and his readers arrive at a high level of understanding of our methods here in Spain. He wanted to give a practical work tool for all parents, players, and coaches, to make their job easier, approaching and making understandable the Spanish teaching system.

I highly recommend *The Secrets of Spanish Tennis* to all parents, coaches, and players who are interested in learning the Spanish methods.

FOREWORD – Emilio Sánchez

When Pato Alvarez left us in January of 2022, it was, for me, a big loss because he shaped my career, guided me and taught me how to live the tennis life, breathe tennis, eat tennis, and sleep tennis. For the tennis industry it was a huge loss because he left one of the strongest tennis legacies with his training method and way of convincing about his beliefs. He revolutionized the way to train tennis in Spain and around the world, and he was a pioneer on how to become a professional player. He invented the famous CUBOS, chains of drills with a purpose, with the goal to repeat as many balls as the CUBO (basket of balls) creating right habits on the footwork to allow any kind of style to be successful, and excel on the chances. This approach, later on in time, became defined as the Spanish system.

Emilio Sánchez

The Secrets of Spanish Tennis does an excellent job explaining the Spanish system and also helps to preserve the legacy of Pato Álvarez and his work. Chris Lewit has studied the Spanish approach for many years, and he is an expert on the drills, methods, and philosophies that Spain has used to build so many champions. In the book he talks about the influence of Pato and shares many of his most famous drills.

People think the system makes the style of the player—but they are wrong. The system has to allow any type of player to improve and excel, and that was Pato's method. Sergio Casal and I both trained with him, and our styles were like the opposite poles. Pato's way allowed us both to arrive at our ceiling as players.

The Spanish method is defined by what the Spanish players have shown the last 40 years. Pato's students starting from Jose Higueras, Angel Gimenez, Lorenzo Fargas, Duarte, Perlas continuing with Sergio Casal, Aguilera, Tous, my generation with Bardou, De Miguel, Jaite, following with my brother Javier, Tomas Carbonell, Roig, Burillo, Alonso, D. Sánchez, Viloca and later younger players like Bruguera, Costa, Corretja, Moya (who didn't train directly with Pato but they trained with his students like Duarte, Perlas, Fargas and also had his influence)...the list goes on and on. All these Spanish players had one common denominator: the way they moved and the way they lived for the tennis.

And first I would like to start with this key: that all Spanish players live for tennis, breathe tennis and always want to get better. That was Pato's mentality and his biggest success, to make so many players live for the sport and work hard.

Secondly, he taught players to play—but also to coach—and most of the names are the biggest coaches in the modern era. His legacy and the famous double rhythm footwork, to take the ball at the peak, receiving the ball, and other tenets were all his commandments.

Pato—above all else—was a character, so convinced that he was always right that no one could contradict him. He grew up in a very difficult environment in Medellin, Colombia, South America. His mother was Catholic and Indian, and his father was Arab and Jewish. He started as a ball boy—that is how he started playing—then played for more than ten years on the tour at the same time he was already coaching. Then in retirement he stayed in Spain coaching initially in a club where I met him, and afterwards in the Spanish federation. He stayed in Spain—but as a foreigner he was never fully recognized or accepted—so he decided to do it all by himself. He used to tell everyone, "I'm the best coach in the world and no one can match me."

In his book, *El Guru Del Tenis,* he tells so many of his commandments—but for me the first one is that he loved the tennis, and he transmitted that love to everyone around him.

Tennis will miss you William, but don't worry because we at Emilio Sánchez Academies will always be grateful for everything you taught us, and we will continue trying to show that love to everyone that comes to Barcelona, Naples and now Dubai.

INTRODUCTION

Spanish tennis or the Spanish method has become synonymous with world-class tennis success in the past thirty or more years.

What makes Spanish tennis so unique? What exactly are those Spanish coaches doing so differently to develop superstars that other systems are not doing? These are the main questions to be answered in this book. *The Secrets of Spanish Tennis* is the culmination of almost 20 years of study about the Spanish way of training. I have visited many of the top Spanish academies and studied with and interviewed some of the leading coaches in Spain to discern and distill this unique and special training methodology.

First of all, some of Spanish success is not really due to a teaching methodology at all. While this book outlines six of the key secrets of Spanish tennis that I believe are the main drivers of Spanish success, there are other important paradigmatic elements, systematic drivers of success that first need to be explained.

Miguel Crespo, leading Spanish sport science researcher, coach, and head of the ITF research office based in Spain, explains that the following elements contribute to Spanish success:

1. The History
2. Tournament Structure
3. Strong Coach Education
4. Competitive Club System
5. Weather
6. Clay Courts
7. Role Models and Mentoring
8. Intensity and Hard Work (both coaches and players)

Let's discuss each of these advantages point by point:

1. The History

The Spanish have a proud tennis culture and believe strongly in honor and tradition. They've had many Grand Slam tournament champions, from Manuel Alonso in the early 1920s to Manuel Santana in the 1960s, and Andres Gimeno and Manuel Orantes in the 1970s. Starting with Sergi Bruguera and then Carlos Moyá (who was the first Spanish man to reach the No. 1 ranking in the 1990s, Juan Carlos Ferrero (who also reached No. 1), Rafael Nadal in the 2000s (one of the greatest players of all time), and then the fast-rising sensation Carlos Alcaraz (who also reached No. 1 in 2022), young Spanish players have a tradition of champions that makes them believe that it is indeed possible to be the best in the world and win major titles. There is also a strong tradition of work ethic and sportsmanship that permeates training models and tennis culture in Spain. All students are expected to give their best, fight, and to win with honor and integrity.

2. Tournament Structure

Spain has one of the best, most comprehensive schedules of national junior, International Tennis Federation (ITF) junior and professional circuits of events of any country in the world. Many top coaches have impressed upon me how important it is to have so many events, both pro and junior, all within driving distance from one another, or a short flight or train ride away. This cluster of high level junior and professional tournaments is a tremendous developmental advantage and can make the move up the junior ITF and professional rankings more manageable and convenient for the players. Also, coaches are able to travel more frequently to watch their players because events are close to home. It is possible to play just professional circuits the whole year in Spain, all within a close radius of Barcelona, for example, without ever getting on a plane. Spain's central European location makes traveling to other European events very convenient as well. Barcelona has direct flights with destinations all over the world from its international airport, which has made it a very popular home base for many ATP/ WTA professionals.

As former world No. 1 doubles player Sergio Casal, co-founder of the Sánchez-Casal Academy (now the Emilio Sánchez

SECRETS OF SPANISH TENNIS 2.0

Academy) told me, in Spain, we have the three things that a player needs to improve: coaches, tournaments, and players. And now more than ever before, everybody is coming here to Spain…The best thing is to have the three things together. You don't find many places with that."

Stefan Ortega, current director of Emilio Sánchez Academy, concurs and believes that the coastal region of Spain and north along the Mediterranean coast to Nice, France is one the greatest areas for tennis in the world, rivaled perhaps only by Florida.

3. Strong Coach Education

Spain has a strong grassroots system with a good coaching education program in place. The RPT, founded by Luis Mediero, is a private coach education provider while the RFET (Spanish Federation) also offers strong beginner to advanced high performance level courses that were greatly shaped by the ideas and methods of Lluis Bruguera and Pato Alvarez. Many of the leading academies have very strong internal coach education programs for their staff, and this is how great coaches in Spain often learn the high performance trade, along with getting their certifications.

4. Competitive Club System

Spain has many strong local club programs and the clubs offer interleague competition teams which serve to help identify young, competitive kids who may have the talent to play the game at a high level. Spain has always had elite wealthy clubs in some of the large cities like Barcelona, but a larger and more rural network of clubs was originally developed and funded in the late 1960s and 1970s by the dictator Franco, who believed that tennis was á good sport for the common people of Spain. Many professional players came through the club system, even starting as ball boys, like Pato Alvarez, Manolo Santana, Manuel Orantes, and Jose Higueras, to name a few.

5. Weather

The weather is similar to Florida, with sun year-round and mild temperatures in winter. Minimal rainfall allows outdoor play on the red clay year-round, which is a major advantage for Spanish players. The hot months of July and August and the generally warm climate help toughen players physically and prepare them for the grind of long matches outdoors. Players in southern Spain train in even hotter climates than those in Barcelona. Although the courts in Madrid are faster due to the high elevation there, the courts play very slow along the coastal areas at sea level.

Sergio Casal perhaps described it best: "What happens here? It's windy. It's sunny. It's hot. And it's slow...And you have to play. You get strong here. Here you can build everything."

In search of better weather and training conditions, Andy Murray famously came to Spain at a young age to train at the then Sánchez-Casal Academy—and many other young British hopefuls have since followed. Marat Safin came to Spain at an early age to hone his game on the red clay, originally to the now defunct TennisVal Academy in Valencia. Many other Russians and Eastern European players have followed him, including Marat's sister Dinara, Igor Andreev, Andrey Rublev and Karen Khachanov, who developed their games at the 4Slam Academy in Barcelona. Garbine Muguruza arrived from Portugal to train for many years at the now closed Bruguera Academy, also in Barcelona. Felix Auger-Aliassime and Casper Ruud are two more examples of players who honed their games in Spain, in their instances at the Rafa Nadal Academy in Mallorca. These are just a few names of the many who, over the years and currently, train in Spain. Because of its great weather, and the many other factors detailed here, of course, Spain is arguably the most popular training base in the world and home to many top European and international juniors and pros.

6. Clay Courts

"We play a lot on clay in Spain because we have a lot of clay courts and it's good for learning the game," said Javier Piles, long-time coach of David Ferrer, the 2013 French Open singles finalist. "On clay the players learn to move and hit their shots on balance even when they are under pressure and this helps them a lot."

The ubiquitous red clay courts of Spain are perhaps the true "Secret" of Spanish tennis. As all Spanish coaches will testify – the clay helps the development of tennis players in myriad ways:

1. The clay in Spain is generally very slow, and by slowing down the ball speed, it becomes very difficult to hit clean winners when kids are young. Young players learn to win with consistency and patience rather than by trying to go for outright

winners. Therefore the clay tends to reward defense and helps to tame hyper-aggressiveness. In Spain, young players learn quickly to play mature, responsible and balanced tennis rather than impulsive, aggressive tennis.

2. Because the points are longer and slower, players learn tactics better. They learn how to construct points rather than just hit winners. Players learn how to position their opponent, hurt them, move them around, and use the geometry of the court. They learn the chess game of tennis.

3. The clay is less stressful on the joints of the lower body and the back, allowing players to train longer and play more with less pain and fewer chronic injuries. The courts are soft and cushion the legs and back from the incessant pounding they receive in tennis. This is a frequently underappreciated aspect of clay court training that is very beneficial to players.

4. The slow ball speed on clay can assist in the development of proper technique in young, developing players. The balls generally don't bounce too high or too fast promoting good grips and contact points for 10-and-under players, and the extra time produces a lot of long rallies for good quality stroke production repetitions. Therefore in Spain, the red, orange green progression that American families are very familiar with (and often frustrated with) here in the US, is not commonplace.

5. The slow and heavy conditions on the red clay force the player to maximize kinetic chain and racquet speed development in order to successfully compete. Players learn by necessity to

develop a strong acceleration or they simply will not be able to attack well and win points. Many people don't realize that the clay can accumulate on the balls and add significant weight in grams to each ball. Hitting a literally heavier ball makes the musculature more strong and powerful over time. The weight of the clay on the ball is reminiscent of the old coach's trick to help develop power by dunking balls in a bucket of water before drills to make them heavier.

6. The inherent instability of the clay surface helps players develop better dynamic balance, stability on the run, and general lower body and foot coordination. Just as hockey players and ice skaters develop strong legs and fantastic balance and agility, so do tennis players who spend significant time on the slippery clay. In fact, in Spain the skill of sliding is often called "skating."

7. Unexpected bounces on the clay develop reactive capabilities, hand-eye coordination, and technical adaptability—sharpening the mind and nervous system. In addition, high bouncing balls help develop strength above the shoulder. Many do not realize that developing this last split-second swing adaptability is a big asset for clay court trained players, no matter what surface they play on. Moreover, muscular strength and endurance on shoulder height balls is critical for players if they want to succeed on clay. Hard court players tend to strike the ball at lower heights. Those hard court players who have not been exposed to clay often feel fatigued in clay court matches because they are not accustomed to striking the ball frequently at higher contact points.

8. Because the points tend to be longer and the matches are often tough grinds, players develop strong character attributes. The clay helps teach competitors to control emotions under fatigue, fight, endure pain, and to manage suffering. For these reasons, Spanish players are often known as the best fighters in any tournament.

9. Due to the slow courts and longer points, players develop better general cardiovascular stamina and muscular endurance. The physical endurance of Spanish players has become legendary.

7. Role Models and Mentoring

During my travels in Spain, I was very surprised at the relative cooperation and friendliness between the elite coaches and academies. Even though they are competitors, they each understand their role in Spanish tennis development and work together when possible to help Spain. As mentioned in the Acknowledgements, some academies and coaches are more guarded and secretive than in the past, but most understand that when Spain rises as a whole all the Spanish academies and coaches prosper.

The same inter-academy cooperation and support is also demonstrated by the individual players in Spain, who are in general, very humble and down to earth, and willing to help their compatriots succeed. There is a "rising tide lifts all boats" mentality, rather than a "scorched earth" competitive approach. Role models and mentoring are an important component to Spanish success. Emilio Sánchez called this the importance of "generations." Spanish players believe in helping the next generation of players to improve Spanish tennis as a whole. Time and again at Spanish training centers, I've seen older pros training with younger junior players without whining or complaining. The Spanish have somehow inculcated this generous nature towards countrymen in the majority of its successful players. "We (in Spain) are like a family and we always try to help each other as much as we can," said well-known Spanish coach Javier Piles.

As former world No. 2 Alex Corretja said to journalist James Goodall, "We are like a family and we always try to help each other as much as we can. When I started, a lot of the top players like Alberto Berasategui and Carlos Costa helped me to become a good player by letting me share coaches and practices with them. I learned a lot from them as a player, and now with this knowledge and my experience, I'm trying to do the same as a coach with the players I work with."

The mentoring approach was adopted not only by players, but by coaches, like Pato Alvarez and Lluis Bruguera, who were open and eager to share their knowledge with the younger generation of talented coaches. That knowledge also became part of the RFET national coaching curriculum and was propagated around the country in workshops, conferences, and certification courses. Pato, before his passing, was always promoting and sharing his system, and Lluis, even to this day, is still happy to discuss his unique training ideas with any coaches who come to visit him. The Emilio Sánchez Academy, and many others like Global Tennis, even offer coach training courses. Emilio Sánchez Academy's course, for example, is offered in conjunction with the RPT to teach any coach who is interested in their specific brand of the "Spanish Method."

Alex Corretja

When I asked Sergio Casal why they offer such a certification course, he stated earnestly that they really wanted to help improve tennis around the world by sharing their system, which is based on the philosophy and methods of Pato Alvarez. Coming from the hypercompetitive world of high performance tennis in the United States, this statement really left an impression on me.

In Goodall's article "Spain's Generation Game" published on the ATP World Tour's website, he described Spain's commitment to helping the next generation for both coaches and players:

"Then, the same situation triggered the next generation; younger coaches learning from older ones, they see the results,

they imitate, and they keep on progressing and so a successful system was formed."

One of the products of that system, 1998 and 2001 Roland Garros finalist Corretja, stressed it wasn't only the coaches who were key, however, but that the older, more experienced and higher-ranked players themselves also fulfilled an important role by mixing with the juniors at that time.

"This is very important in the development of the younger players," said Corretja. "When I was young I was lucky enough to practice with players like Emilio Sánchez and Carlos Costa as well as many others and it was unbelievable for me as I was dying to get on the court with them. When I was a little bit older I used to practice with some of the younger players coming through, like Carlos Moya and Juan Carlos Ferrero, and now the young guys in Spain are practicing with them so it works really well."

Having benefited from the system himself, the belief that older players have a duty to nurture young talent wasn't lost on Moya, who famously took Rafael Nadal under his wing when the Mallorcan was a young teenager taking his first tentative steps on the professional circuit.

"I got to know Carlos way before I started playing on the tour and I practiced with him a lot back home in Mallorca," said Nadal. "I trusted him and he gave me a lot of confidence."

Spain's focus on blending the generations not only provides mentoring support for players but also helps to reinforce the competitive spirit. Said Albert Costa, the 2002 French Open champion, "The role models are very important here in Spain. Where we train I have (Albert) Montañes, (Nicolas) Almagro, (Feliciano) Lopez, a lot of professional tennis players and they practice with the young players. They play with them. For the juniors it's good to see the difference of the levels. It's very, very important."

Thus the unusual amount of inter-academy cooperation, coach and player mentoring and role modeling, and friendly competition between compatriots has been an incredible asset to Spanish tennis development as a whole. Other countries looking to learn from the success of Spain would be wise to encourage a similar culture of generosity, humility, sharing and cooperation.

8. Intensity and Hard Work (both coaches and players)

Albert Costa summed this up perfectly when he said, "The most important thing with drills is the intensity. If you make drills with intensity, full of concentration, that's the only way you can improve your tennis." This mentality is evident throughout Spanish tennis.

Said Spanish coach Alberto Lopez, "The most important thing is the mentality. We are really fierce... This is our game." Spanish players are legendary for their work ethic, grit, and endurance, as these coaches attest. The intensity and hard work is a simple reason for Spain's success that is sometimes overlooked in the search for a more esoteric explanation. Spanish players and coaches in the last 30 years or more have simply outworked the rest of the world, and this has been a huge factor in the country's success.

Thus, these eight contributing factors — all coaching philosophies and methods aside — have been tremendously important in Spain's rise to dominance in the tennis world. Before focusing on the Secrets themselves, it will help the reader to have some background on the history of Spanish tennis.

A Brief History of Spanish Tennis

Andres Gimeno   Manuel Orantes

In 1973, there were only two Spaniards among the ATP top 50: Manuel Orantes and Andrés Gimeno. In 1989 there were five Spanish players in the top 100: Emilio Sánchez, Sergi Bruguera, Jordi Arrese, Javier Sánchez-Vicario, and, and Tomás Carbonell. In 2011, the number of Spanish players inside the Top 50 had more than quadrupled from two to nine, while the nation boasted a staggering 13 in the Top 100. In addition, 19 (and counting) Spaniards have joined the Top 10 since the ATP rankings began in 1973. In addition, Spain has won the Davis Cup six times since 2000 and the Fed Cup five times in the 1990s.

By 2016, Spain had a record 15 players in the top 100 ATP, however, many of the top Spanish players were getting older and journalists and observers both in and outside of Spain were worried that Spanish tennis could struggle in the future with nobody to replace the older guard. Coaches and tennis industry leaders in Spain were very concerned, but by 2023 the explosion of Carlos Alcaraz to No. 1 and the steady improvement of Pablo Carreno-Busta into the top 10 have buttressed the continued miraculous success of the seemingly ageless Rafael Nadal. In addition, many new solid talents from Spain have emerged into the top 100 and the success of Paola Badosa, who rose to No. 2 in the world on the women's side of the game, all means the future is still bright for Spanish tennis. On the juniors front, Martin Landaluce, the 2022 US Open junior champion, leads the next generation of hungry and talented Spanish players. While Spain may not have 15 top 100 ATP players perennially for the next decade, they should have a solid number, and Alcaraz holds the promise to carry the mantle for Nadal at the top of the world.

So how exactly has Spain, a very small country, developed into a dominant tennis force in just a handful of decades?

In the 1960s, Spanish tennis was flat and slice old school style, like most other parts of the world. The Spanish were consistent, patient, and good on clay. Often they were described (in a derogatory fashion) as baseline pushers. Manuel (Manolo) Santana was the first great Spanish player of the late 20th century, winning four major singles titles: Wimbledon, the French and U.S. titles in the 1960s. He won the French

Championships in 1961 and 1964, the U.S. Championships in 1965 and Wimbledon in 1966. Santana was inducted into the International Tennis Hall of Fame in 1984. Andres Gimeno won the French in 1972 and was inducted in the International Tennis Hall of Fame in 2009. Manuel Orantes won the U.S. Open in 1975 and reached a career high No. 2 in the world. Orantes was later inducted into the International Tennis Hall of Fame in 2012.

Santana was very popular in Spain, captivated the people, and drew the attention of the dictator Francisco Franco. General Franco was a tennis fan and he believed tennis could be a great sport for the proletariat in Spain—not just the wealthy aristocracy in Barcelona and other cities. He believed tennis could be a boon to the people, and a vehicle to better health and fitness and country pride.

Manolo Santana

In the 1960s and until his death in 1975, Franco supported the establishment of tennis clubs around the country both financially and with his governmental powers and policies. The rise of tennis popularity in Spain coincided with what scholars call The Spanish Miracle, (*el milagro español*), which refers to a period of sustained economic growth and prosperity in Spain. Therefore, it is deeply ironic that this harsh dictator who brought so much death and destruction to Spain and oppressed his people also helped create economic prosperity and the foundation for world tennis dominance that has brought great success and esteem to Spain.

After Franco's passing, the country moved towards democracy and the Spanish people received new freedoms. The economy was steadily growing, and as democracy and hope flourished among the people in Spain, so did the hopes of young children to play tennis and become champions of the world. Grand Slam tennis success for Spain, however, would take a long time to achieve.

After Orantes's triumph at Forest Hills (on clay, by the way), and the death of Franco, both in 1975, there was a long 18-year Grand Slam tournament title drought for Spain on the men's side. During that period, Spain still produced a handful of strong players like Jose Higueras, who reached No. 6 in the world in 1983. The dry spell was broken when Sergi Bruguera triumphed at the 1993 and 1994 French Open titles back to back. Arantxa Sánchez-Vicario did win the French Open on the women's side during that time—in 1989 – and she went on to forge a Hall of Fame career winning four major titles in all (three at Roland Garros, one at the U.S. Open) and achieved the No. 1 singles and doubles ranking. The Bruguera 1993 Roland Garros victory had a very special meaning and a deep psychological positive impact on the tennis culture in Spain. The victory was an earth-shattering moment and ended the seemingly interminable men's Grand Slam aridity. The influence of the Bruguera Grand Slam tournament breakthrough cannot be overstated and helped a generation of players to believe that big-time tennis success for Spanish players could be possible.

Spain began to have more success at the pro level and more Spanish players started to arrive at the top of the game.

In addition to the success of Arantxa Sánchez-Vicario, Conchita Martínez won at Wimbledon in 1994 and achieved the world No. 2 ranking. Albert Costa won the 2002 French Open and many other Spanish players moved into the top ATP rankings. Carlos Moya, developed by Mallorcan coach Jofre Porta, won the French Open in 1998 and became the first male Spanish player to reach the No. 1 world ranking in 1999. Juan Carlos Ferrero, coached by Antonio Cascales, won the 2003 Roland Garros title and also reached the No. 1 ranking that year. Of course, the greatest Spanish player ever—and possibly the greatest player in tennis history—Rafael Nadal—rose to fame during the early 2000s. Nadal, coached by his uncle Toni Nadal, has eclipsed all other great champions from Spain, having won 14 Roland Garros titles, two Australian Opens, two Wimbledons, and four US Opens, as of the start of 2024.

Arantxa Sánchez-Vicario

Sergi Bruguera

On the women's side, the history of Garbine Muguruza is also notable. Muguruza emigrated from Venezuela at six years old and began training under the mentorship and tutelage of

Luis Bruguera and his team at the Bruguera Academy in Barcelona. She won her first of two major titles in 2016 at Roland Garros and also reached the world No. 1 ranking in 2017 after winning Wimbledon that same year.

Carlos Alcaraz was born in Murcia, Spain in the same year that Juan Carlos Ferrero won Roland Garros and became No. 1 in the world. Less than two decades later in 2022—and coached by Juan Carlos himself—Alcaraz has won the US Open and Wimbledon reached the No. 1 ranking, only the fourth Spanish man to achieve the top world ranking. Alcaraz has had a meteoric, fairy tale ride to the top of the game with the help of Juan Carlos Ferrero, Antonio Cascales, and the entire team at their academy Equelite Juan Carlos Ferrero, in Villena.

Garbine Muguruza

During the 1980s and 1990s Lluis Bruguera (Sergi's father and coach) and William Pato Álvarez had many successful students who reached the top of the world for Spain. This success brought these coaches fame and fortune—and a lot of influence in a small country that had experienced a long period without Grand Slam victories. These hard-working, charismatic coaching titans started to change the way tennis was trained and played in Spain. They taught topspin and powerful forehands, while keeping the historical Spanish focus on consistency and stamina in place. Spanish players were no longer just consistent counter punchers or pushers.

Carlos Moya

Juan Carlos Ferrero

Rafael Nadal

Carlos Alcaraz

The Bruguera style of coaching became prominent in Spain as Lluis's players gained success. Fernando Luna, a protégé of Lluis, reached a career high ranking of No. 33, Jordi Arrese, another Bruguera student reached a career high of No. 23. Sergi Bruguera, however, was able to reach the pinnacle of men's tennis for Spain. Sergi won the Spanish junior nationals in 1987 and rose quickly on the ATP Tour, finishing in the top 30 by 1989. When Sergi (guided by Lluis) broke through in 1993 to become the first Spanish male player in 18 years to win a major singles title (since Orantes), it brought the Bruguera family and teaching system a lot of positive recognition. As mentioned, Sergi Bruguera went on to win Roland Garros twice and reach No. 3 in the world. Curiously, Bruguera is the only ATP player to have a winning record against both Roger Federer and Pete Sampras, and he absolutely inspired a generation of younger Spanish players and coaches:

"When Sergi won the first Grand Slam, the first French Open (since Gimeno in 1972), I think we all started to believe maybe we can do it," said Albert Costa. "A lot of good players were coming up. He won the French Open the same year that I lost in the final of the French Open junior—so for me it was like ... okay, this guy is very good. He can win the French Open. I can play with him. So why can't I? I think when you have somebody close who's able to

Albert Costa

achieve something really unbelievable, you start thinking that you can do it as well."

Pato Alvarez, for his part, at one point in his career was coaching four top 50 ATP players *simultaneously*, (Sergio Casal, Emilio Sánchez, Javier Sánchez, and Franscisco Clavet), a feat that may never be duplicated—in addition to many other great players over his career like Tomas Carbonell, Jordi Burillo, Juan Balcells, Julián Alonso, Carlos Cuadrado and Joan Albert Viloca. Pato's discipline and system of geometric drills from baskets became popular all across Spain and filtered down to the younger generation of coaches throughout the country.

The 1980s and early 1990s were foundational years built by the hard work and dedication of Lluis and Pato, and

Jordi Arrese

a generation of other Spanish coaches who followed their methods or borrowed pieces of their methods. Based on personal interviews, many top Spanish coaches and players have also agreed that the Barcelona Olympics in 1992 had a profound effect on tennis in Spain, and that the Olympics were another important factor in stimulating the continued growth of tennis during the 1990s. Interestingly, a star pupil of Lluis Bruguera, Jordi Arrese, won silver in singles for Spain at that event. The Olympics inspired kids across the country, gave the Spanish Tennis

Federation more money, and spurred tennis infrastructure development all over the country.

It's also important to place Rafa in the timeline. Rafael Nadal was born in 1986 – the same year Lluis Bruguera founded the Bruguera Tennis Academy—and started training with his Uncle Toni Nadal in the early 1990s, about the same time as Sergi Bruguera reclaimed Spanish glory at the Roland Garros. Undoubtedly Toni Nadal was influenced by the successes of the Bruguera and Álvarez methods of training as he sought to develop his nephew into a tennis superstar in the 1990s.

The recent modern tennis era in Spain has given rise to numerous top Spanish players such as Bruguera, Carlos Moyá, Juan Carlos Ferrero, Alex Corretja, Albert Costa and, more recently, Rafael Nadal (one of the greatest players ever, Fernando Verdasco, Nicolas Almagro, Feliciano Lopez, and many others). Spain's newest sensation, Carlos Alcaraz, has electrified the Spanish tennis culture and captivated the sporting public's attention. Spanish women, who have traditionally had less depth than the men in the pro game, are having better success than in the past with Badosa (who reached a career high No. 2 in 2022), Garbine Muguruza, and Sara Sorribes Tormo, for example, all in the top 40 WTA rankings.

On the women's side, there have been some great achievements but not the depth of domination that can be seen with the Spanish men. Questions still linger as to why that is the case. Arantxa Sánchez-Vicaro was an incredible champion and reached No. 1 in the world, Conchita Martinez became the first Spanish woman to win Wimbledon in 1994, and Garbine Muguruza has won two major titles while Badosa reached the No. 2 ranking. These are strong examples of Spanish female players succeeding on the pro tour. Some coaches whom I interviewed in Spain explained that girls sometimes don't get the same level of serious coaching as the boys and that the athletic participation rate in Spain may be higher for boys than girls. These facts could account for some of the differences in results between men and women professionally.

So who was really responsible for the rise of this so-called Spanish Armada? Where were the seeds sown for Spanish success? Lluis Bruguera and Pato Alvarez were there in the trenches in the 1980s and 1990s building the foundation:

"In 1993, Sergi Bruguera became the first Spaniard to win a Grand Slam title since Orantes in 1975 when he triumphed at Roland Garros, and while he was undoubtedly the leading man of his generation, he was ably supported by the likes of 1994 Roland Garros finalist Alberto Berasategui, former Italian Open champion and world No. 7 ranked Emilio Sánchez, and former world No. 10 Carlos Costa," wrote Goodall in an excellent Spanish tennis review found on the ATP's website. "This kind of success was no fluke, however, and it was the coaches working with these players that many credit with sowing the seeds of this Spanish Armada of talent."

"Back in the day there were players like Sergi Bruguera and Emilio Sánchez and their coaches, Pato Alvarez and [Sergi's father] Lluis Bruguera, and they created the feeling that by working the way they worked, it was possible to get better results at the international level," said Jose Perlas, the coach of Nicolas Almagro, to Goodall. "Players at a lower level, as I considered myself to be at that time, understood and learned that they were creating a system and we started to believe it was possible to get really good results. Because coaches worked with younger players, as well, a second generation was achieved; Alex Corretja, Albert Costa, Carlos Moya and Felix Mantilla along with many others at that time."'

In the 1990s, Jofre Porta is an example of a younger generation coach who helped guide Moyá's rise to dominance: "It would be foolish, however, to forget Moya's run to the final in Melbourne back in 1997, which must have helped other Spanish players believe that success at the majors was possible outside Paris," wrote Goodall. "Moya's climb to the summit of the singles rankings in 1999—he was the first Spanish player to achieve the No. 1 ranking—is testament to his adaptability. Becoming the best player in the world is impossible if you can't play extremely well on all surfaces, especially clay and hard courts, given the proliferation of tournaments now held on that surface."

"Carlos is one of the greatest sportsmen that we've ever had," Nadal said to Goodall. "He's a great person and has been a great example to us all. He was a pioneer when he became the first world No. 1 we have had in Spain, and I've been fortunate to know him."

Following Moya's ascent to the No. 1 ranking, Juan Carlos Ferrero also reached the summit of men's tennis for eight weeks in 2003. He had won at Roland Garros and reached the final of the U.S. Open. "When someone Spanish who is close to you gets to No. 1, you think to yourself that if you have a similar level, then you can reach the top, too," Ferrero said to Goodall. "For Spanish tennis, Carlos was the first to become No. 1 and he led the way for others, like myself and Rafa, who learned a lot from him."

Spain has had incredible success in the last few decades developing Spanish-born players, but many do not realize how many great non-Spanish champions Spain has produced during the same time period. In addition, many former Spanish pros are now coaching on the tour or around the world at different academies. Indeed, Sergio Casal's noble goal of improving tennis training around the world with Spanish methods is coming to fruition.

For example, Pancho Alvariño and José Altur at TennisVal Academy (now Lozano-Altur) in Valencia have helped develop foreign players like Marat Safin, Dinara Safina and Igor Andreev, along with homegrown talent David Ferrer. Britain's Andy Murray and Canada's Milos Raonic have also been strong advocates of training in Spain, having moved there to train in their formative years. Murray came to Spain to train with Pato Álvarez. Countless foreign players from all over Europe and beyond flock to Spain to develop their tennis. Most recently, Iga Swiatek and Casper Ruud have trained at the Rafael Nadal Tennis Academy in Mallorca. Milos Raonic, Andrey Rublev and Karen Khachanov are notable players who honed their skills in Barcelona at 4Slam Tennis with former ATP pros and now coaches Fernando Vicente and Galo Blanco. Felix Auger-Aliassime was coached by Toni Nadal; and Alexander Zverev was coached by Sergi Bruguera. The list of tour players coached by former Spanish pros keeps growing. It would be remiss to overlook the profound impact Spanish coach Jose Higueras has had on American tennis since moving to the US in the 1980s. Jose has worked with dozens of American pros and prospects like Michael Chang, Jim Courier, Frances Tiafoe and Coco Gauff. Higueras was instrumental in bringing Spanish philosophy and methods to USTA Player

Development for almost a decade in the mid 2000s. The Spanish method continues to lead as a country producing native champions but also influences countless other players around the world who come to experience and benefit from Spanish tennis training and philosophy.

Andy Murray

Understanding the history of Spanish tennis has given me a profound appreciation for how powerful and successful the system has become, accounting for a dramatic improvement in the world professional rankings of Spanish players, but also of numerous non-native players too.

There has been a dramatic shift in the training protocols that has led to incredible success on the international stage for such a small country with a moderate population. It is important to note the major influences of the older guard, the legends of Spanish tennis: Lluis Bruguera and Pato Alvarez. It seems that almost every younger coach whom I have interviewed has referenced Pato and Lluis, their dynamism, hard work, and the system that they created, which although separate and different, maintain many common elements.

What Spain has accomplished in the last few decades is truly a miracle, and the astute tennis observer should be eager to understand the keys to Spain's success. The following chapters will detail these secrets of Spanish tennis, as I have discerned and distilled them. The goal is to provide a guide for coaches, players and parents to the often confusing world of Spanish tennis by providing explanations, descriptions, and to share important drills and philosophies.

*Part I: The Secrets *

The Secrets of Spanish Tennis are the common core elements that I have observed being taught across the country by different leading academies and coaches. They are the essence of the Spanish way, if the Spanish way can be effectively defined as a universal system.

I have tried to harmonize the many varied and disconnected approaches that can be found across the country into simple elements that all coaches, parents, and players around the world can learn and assimilate into their own training systems. The core Spanish elements are versatile and easily adaptable to or "piggybacked" onto other systems, and indeed this is part of their inherent value. The secrets are so remarkably easy to assimilate that I've often remarked that the Spanish way is like the Buddhism religion, which historically spread rapidly throughout Asia and the rest of the world due to its ease of assimilation and adaptability to other religions. The fact is that systems with intense, strong dogma, whether religious or otherwise, often do not spread as easily as methods that have some flexibility and do not seek to supplant other systems entirely. I have made every effort to highlight commonalities in the Spanish way that can be easily adapted to current systems to provide supplemental support, although of course, these principles could be used to supplant your current training regimens entirely.

It is also important to understand that these six secrets, while they can be taught as independent subjects, are often integrated into complete exercises in Spain. One of the hallmarks of the Spanish way, in general, is that the coaches work *simply*, without an overemphasis on only one area, such as technique, for example. Many of the exercises that are highlighted in this book work with many elements of the player's game in an integrated and holistic way—technical, tactical, physical, and mental all in one exercise combined.

Spain has developed a style of training that is successful in part due to its "keep it simple," holistic approach. In an effort to explain the philosophy and system in Spain, I have necessarily broken the approach into parts, but the reader should remember that the Spanish Way often teaches these six core secrets all-at-once in integrated exercises, many of which will be detailed in the following chapters.

CHAPTER 1

Footwork, Movement, and Balance

"Without balance, a player cannot be consistent and will lose confidence..."
—*Lluis Bruguera*

Footwork is an obsession for Spanish coaches, as well as many South American coaches. The top academies and coaches relentlessly drill their players to move quickly, fluidly, and to get in position.

Why has footwork become such an obsession in Spanish coaching circles? My best guess is that it probably has something to do with a European culture that tends to focus on playing with the feet more than the hands (consider the popularity of soccer in Europe vis-à-vis the popularity of baseball in the

United States), and with a tennis culture that celebrates running and triumphing on the red clay, where footwork is essential to winning. The clay surface itself is like a second teacher, helping to train the movement and balance even without the coach's input or drills.

Any Spanish coach worth his salt will have a toolbox of effective footwork drills (usually hand-fed) that he can use to help a player with positioning work (I will at times use the terms footwork and positioning interchangeably in this chapter and many of these great footwork drills will be documented at the end).

I must admit my own coaching has been greatly enhanced by studying footwork overseas at leading Spanish academies over many years. I have learned the keys to positioning, moving quickly with balance, and recovering, and I have picked up many unique and super drills along the way. Indeed, here in the U.S. I have become known as a go-to leading expert on footwork and movement, with players coming from around the country to train with me. There is high demand for high level footwork training. Many of the skills that I'm teaching in my footwork method are Spanish based. The essential skills that are fundamental to moving well on clay in Spain seem to be sorely needed here in the U.S. and in other countries around the world.

I enjoy sharing the Spanish approach to movement and footwork because I believe Spanish coaches have developed some very important pedagogical approaches and drills to develop this key area. I think all coaches could learn how to teach movement and footwork better by studying the Spanish way. Parents can also benefit by understanding the movement patterns, footwork and philosophy better to help their kids. Players can learn how to play well and move comfortably in all areas of the court, even the far recesses.

To begin to explain the secrets of Spanish footwork, I would like to start by explaining what Spanish coaches look for when a player moves.

Balance

A player needs to move fluidly with dynamic balance and good posture. Posture is very important to the Spanish coach. Controlling the COG (center of gravity) is also very important.

Spanish coaches are trained to look for imbalances when the player is on the move, during the shot, and on the recovery. Sometimes a player must shift his or her COG, in order to move quickly to a shot (for example, when sprinting to a ball out wide), but more often than not, and especially during the actual shot itself, the body should be centered with the trunk upright. Rotation should take place around a central axis. Spanish coaches also tend to focus on the head position of the player during movement to and from the ball—and especially during the swing itself. The head should remain stable during the swing, particularly when swinging fast with maximum acceleration. In Spain, the coaches are obsessed with the stability of the head because if the head flails about wildly it will corrupt the balance of the body and the control of the shot itself. Spanish coaches understand that controlling the head is the key to controlling the rest of the body and ultimately controlling the ball. Even the extension through the ball—the swing path—can be negatively affected by too much head movement. Therefore, the stability of the head is critical in the Spanish method and Spanish coaches always look for a "quiet' head during the swing.

Three Metrics To Control The Contact Point

Spanish coaches are obsessed with managing the contact point, or the relationship between the body and the incoming ball. Firstly, Spanish coaches look for the contact point to be at the right height. In Spain, the most frequent directive to describe this is translated: "hit the ball between your hip and shoulder." In other words, don't let the ball drop below your hips or bounce over your shoulders where it's out of the strike zone (to borrow an American baseball term). Thus the height of the struck ball should be between the hip and the shoulder for the majority of shots.

Secondly, the distance between the body and the ball needs to be optimized to avoid cramping of the arm or arms during the forward swing. This measurement relates prominently to the technical goal of good extension, which I wrote about at length in my technique book, *Winning Pretty*. In Spain, this distance management is often called "measuring the ball." If the player has arrived and managed the distance well, the measurement should be good, and he or she will be able to extend the racquet and "accompany the ball," as Toni Nadal likes to say, outward on the correct swing path. Lluis Bruguera calls this "following the *line* of the shot." The correct measurement leads to better control of the ball.

Thirdly, the body should be positioned such that the ball is played early and out in front. One of the most commonly used footwork teaching phrases in Spain is translated as: "get (your body/feet) behind the ball," used by Spanish coaches to instruct their players to get into position with their bodies so that the ball can be played out in front. This is another important aspect of measuring the ball well and also helps allow good extension of the arm or arms. An early impact point in front of the body also allows the player to generate more racquet speed, spin and power by producing better energy transfer through hip and trunk rotation. This racquet speed generation by meeting the ball correctly out in front is critical to the Spanish method and will be discussed more in Chapter 2.

When the three criteria above are met, the Spanish coach is happy because the body has a better chance to be on balance during the delivery of the shot if the contact point is correct. However, if the contact point is not correct—if even one criterion is missing—the player will most likely lose control of his COG and be off balance for the shot. The player could lose racquet speed and the accompaniment of the ball, which is anathema to the Spanish approach.

Therefore, there is a critical connection between the contact point, the balance, and the footwork; they are intertwined and woven together. Ultimately, the positioning of the player's feet determines whether the contact point is good, and thus whether the shot will be in balance or not. Spanish coaches become obsessed with the positioning because, without it, there is often a bad contact point and usually poor balance.

Positioning

Positioning in Spain classically means getting behind the incoming ball and getting the feet in a good stance (often called the "support system") while maintaining the optimal distance measurement from the ball. The goal of good positioning is to allow for a balanced body during the swing for the most consistent, powerful, and accurate shot possible. Positioning can also mean court position (such as whether a player is playing deep in the backcourt or close to the baseline). In this case, Spanish coaches guide players to be in the right position to attack or defend, depending on the situation and the type of a ball hit by the opponent. The positioning, as per the first definition, can be thought of as the footwork used to "receive the ball," a commonly used phrase in Spanish tennis teaching. Receiving the ball means getting the feet into the right position to allow a good, balanced reception of the incoming flight of the ball, like an outfielder getting back behind a fly ball (to use another baseball analogy). In Spain there is an obsession with reading the ball with the eyes and then getting the footwork right during the flight of the incoming ball. In other words, Spanish coaches are obsessed with how their players receive the ball. Players must receive the ball properly, in a good position, set up a stable support system with the legs, and then send the ball while maintaining that balance and stability.

Based on my experience studying tennis systems in the United States, I sincerely believe that our coaching curriculums do not spend nearly enough time working on footwork and especially this critical skill—the positioning—as they should. Fortunately, José Higueras (a well-known Spanish coach and former top 10 player himself), during his tenure as Director of Coaching for USTA Player Development, worked very hard to teach American coaches how to develop the footwork and positioning of their players. In fact, the USTA has adopted many Spanish philosophies and even many Spanish footwork drills in its updated teaching methodology, which is promoted to U.S. coaches. One major teaching thrust that Jose has brought from Spain is the conceptual framework of Eyes/Mind—Feet—Hands. The construct means that players first must receive the ball well by reading the incoming flight (Eyes and Mind) and adjusting the body (Feet). Players must then send the ball with a correct biomechanical swing with good racquet acceleration (Hands). This model has been an important part of the USTA High Performance coaching philosophy since Jose became director.

José Higueras

The USTA has also installed more red clay courts at their national training centers and even imported Italian red dirt for the USTA National Campus at Lake Nona, Florida (which was very expensive to do, by the way!). The USTA also sends top American players to Barcelona Total Tennis to train on the red dirt and prepare for clay court events in Europe (also expensive). It's very clear that the USTA has wholeheartedly and earnestly invested in training the Spanish way by embracing and promoting playing on clay!

What stance should players use as they get into position? In Spain, believe it or not, many academies still stress the basic neutral stance (which I see as almost an anachronism in the modern game, but the traditional neutral stance is still highly favored and is often recommended especially for beginners, which I think is good advice). Bruguera Academy used to do this before it closed, and Emilio Sánchez Academy (ESA) is also a major proponent of this classical approach, for example. ESA still teaches neutral stance and stepping into the ball as the foundational footwork skill. However, new modern academies like the Rafa Nadal Academy (RNA) in Mallorca take a different approach. The legendary Spanish coach Toni Nadal is the director there and he believes firmly in teaching advanced players to jump and leave the ground by exploding up into the ball. While Toni does teach the classical closed stance to younger beginning students, as students advance in level they are encouraged to go airborne—but always with balance and good body control!

That being said, it is clear that most Spanish players evolve to use semi-open and open stances, and they use these heavily at the top ITF and professional levels. These stances are certainly acceptable for higher level players and situationally, on emergency balls out wide, for example. Open stance can be used to get more body rotation and thus more racquet speed, power, and spin as players advance in level. No matter what the stance, the positioning must be there, and the balance must be maintained through the shot.

It's worth mentioning that great positioning, in the Spanish system, is linked with what Spanish coaches like Lluis Bruguera and others call "reading." Reading is using the eyes to see the tactical situation unfolding on the other side of the net and observing the flight of the incoming ball. Spanish coaches generally work on the reading skills together with the footwork skills, because without good reading the player cannot position his or her body effectively and efficiently. As legendary Spanish coach Jose Higueras said, "We must train the eyes and the feet together." Thus reading and positioning using the eyes and feet are inextricably linked in the Spanish approach.

Quickness and Stamina of Movement

In Spain, the quickness of the movement is important, but I would say that stamina—the ability to make movements over and over again with precision—is the more fundamental style of footwork training on the tennis court. The footwork teaching that I have observed of a classical, "older-school" Spanish coach like Pato Alvarez, tended to emphasize long sets of rhythmic movements rather than short bursts (Alvarez and his teaching methodology will be profiled in Chapter 7; also see Tennisplayer magazine article "Two Geniuses," available at www.chrislewit.com or www.tennisplayer.net). Younger generation and more modern coaches like Toni Nadal and Jofre Porta from Mallorca, by contrast, emphasized shorter bursts of work training quickness more than long repetitive stamina sets.

Toni Nadal and his team at Rafa Nadal Academy prefer to work in shorter sequences of 6-20 balls rather than long sets of movement repetitions common in the Bruguera method at the Bruguera Academy or Emilio Sánchez Academy, which teaches the Pato Alvarez method. At those schools, many of the footwork and movement exercises are slow and rhythmic in nature, droning on at a slower cadence and often lasting dozens of repetitions. Antonio Cascales and his team at Ferrero Tennis Academy offer a blend of classical and modern training with some longer aerobic drills and shorter anaerobic bursting type movement exercises. Jordi Vilaró and Francis Roig, at Barcelona Total Tennis, train their players with a similarly blended approach as JC Ferrero.

Therefore perhaps there is some *changing of the guard* going on in Spain currently, where the techniques of the legends like Pato and Lluis Bruguera, the guys who built the Spanish Armada are evolved as some of the relatively younger coaches like Nadal, Porta, and others take center stage. This evolution must happen in every country and with every system as new coaching gurus become more prominent and "legends" fade out of the spotlight or retire. In my experience traveling to some of the most well-known academies in Spain, most Spanish movement training is still more stamina based, with longer sets of 20-60 balls of repetitions. Alvarez and Bruguera work this way. Bruguera also offers some shorter, quick movement drills in his method as well. Porta works in the repetition range of 4-8 balls generally when he is training footwork, so there is some variation depending on the individual coach. Jose Higueras, in a private interview, stated that he likes to work in repetition ranges of 8-15, or up to 20 repetitions during clay court preparation periods. Higueras said, "I don't think the longer repetitions that are sometimes done in Spain are necessary." Obviously, Lluis and Pato would disagree with that sentiment.

Lluis Bruguera's method works a combination of both ranges, with more emphasis on balance and positioning than pure quickness, although he has some drills that are shorter duration for quickness. Alvarez doesn't work many sharp movements or quick changes of direction at all. I once asked him if he felt working on those movement skills were important on the court, and he demurred, explaining that the double rhythm steps were more important. In fact, Pato seemed to be obsessed more with training the double rhythm footwork steps and the X pattern—which he created and made famous—with near exclusivity. Don't get me wrong, most Spanish coaches want quick, sharp, adroit footwork movements, but they will leave it to the physical trainer to develop. I have not observed a preponderance of Spanish coaches systematically and regularly training for physical speed improvement *on the tennis court*, although some speed improvement is expected from any technical efficiencies gained. Most of the coaches around the country, by and large, seem to have adopted the Alvarez and Bruguera approach and leave the multidirectional speedwork to the off-court physical trainer.

When drills hit the repetition range above 10 balls, the player begins to work sub-maximally and aerobically rather than at a maximum and anaerobically, which is where physical speed improvement comes from at near full sprint speed and involving many sharp changes of direction. Consequently, in the classic Spanish footwork system, the quickness of the footwork is often left to the physical trainer to improve. In the classic Spanish footwork system, the coach is training balance and positioning rhythmically and aerobically, rather than anaerobically—think sets of 10 to 30 or more balls at medium intensity rather than 4-10 balls at highest intensity. This is the method and influence of Pato and Lluis.

In this way, stamina is clearly trained at the same time as movement and balance. The player must have great endurance to perform the movements over and over again with good footwork technique and balance. Of course, the extra stamina training comes in handy when the player is facing a tough third or fifth set at Roland Garros. The combination of on court slow and rhythmic stamina type drills and off-court multidirectional speed work with the physical trainer has been successful over the past decades in Spain and could be a good model for other countries to follow. The approach doesn't seem to hinder or stifle the on-court movement or speed development of the players, builds incredible stamina, and enhances movement technique, all while keeping the risk of an on-court training injury very low.

Anticipation/Reaction

Anticipation and reaction are two facets of movement and footwork that are trained quite frequently in Spain, and they both contribute to overall quickness to the ball. Spanish coaches like to train the eyes to read the situation, picking up the ball early—anticipation—and they like to train the neuromuscular connection, the signal from the eyes to the brain to the feet—reaction. In addition, good reading of the tactical situation and how it affects court positioning are frequently focused on during racquet feeding and live ball exercises, including during point play. According to Lluis Bruguera, "If before the ball is shot, you can't anticipate; if you open angles and you don't cover the court, your opponent has advantage." For him, it's obvious: "If you are in a good position to hit your shot, the results are completely different. To arrive in that position you need to learn two things: read (with the eyes) and go."

This type of training is usually performed in quick bursts and for shorter duration in contrast to the slower, high volume work discussed above. The bulk of the movement training across the country is more slow and rhythmic with small amounts of quick, eyes and reaction training interspersed into practices. To train the anticipation and the reaction specifically, coaches will hand toss feeds in quick, random patterns and will try to disguise the tosses so as to surprise the player. The player is forced to use his eyes to read the coach's hands and to anticipate the next feed. Jofre Porta is a master of this type of footwork training—and so is Bruguera. Toni Nadal likes to train the eyes and reaction with fast racquet fed balls from across the net. I will give a few examples of these types of drills at the end of the chapter, and we will put all the footwork drills on my website, SecretsofSpanishTennis.com, and the Chris Lewit Tennis YouTube channel for readers to view.

It's important to note that—no matter what the exercise or game—Spanish coaches are obsessed with the eyes, reaction, and a good footwork response to position the player well to receive the ball. This contrasts with methods from other countries that focus more on technical movements of footwork and swing mechanics. In Spain, too much technical discussion or dissection is discouraged and tracking, reading, and responding to the flight of the incoming ball are heavily prioritized. In addition, the tactical situation and decision making are integrated into the footwork and movement drills, which help players grow their mind and tactical awareness in concert with improving their eyes (reading) and feet (positioning). Therefore, the concept of anticipation in Spain is multilayered and does not only connote seeing the incoming ball well, but also relates to understanding the strategic options for every given situation.

> *"I think the most important system in Spanish tennis is first the footwork (to move with more anticipation when the ball is coming, to be in perfect position for more acceleration and more control), the speed, acceleration with the racquet (we take the racquet very strong with the fingers, but the wrist relaxed like Nadal), and also to be very consistent players."*
> —Fernando Luna, former top 35 ATP player and former head coach at the Bruguera Academy

Feeding From The Hand

All differences aside, in Spain, hand feeding of footwork drills seems to be almost universally accepted as the best way to develop the footwork and balance. The coach has more control of the speed and timing of the feed, can communicate better with the player, and can see the technique of the movements more clearly by being close to the player when hand feeding. The method of Toni Nadal presents an exception to the hand feeding rule. Toni favors racquet feeding, but still uses hand feeding with less frequency than other legendary coaches in Spain. Pato Alvarez was famous for using his racquet to tap balls to players from the same side of the net rather than tossing the ball from his hand. In a personal interview, Pato explained that he believed it was better for the player's eyes and reading if he or she saw the ball coming off the strings of the coach's racquet as opposed to reacting to a hand fed ball.

360 Degree Movements

In Spain, footwork is taught in 360 degree movements, rather than just laterally and forward. In my experience, most American coaches teach 180 degree movement—lateral and forward—to attack. Rafael Nadal is the prototypical Spanish runner, with great speed, anticipation, footwork and positioning, stamina, and willingness to chase down any ball. Carlos Alcaraz also demonstrates a wonderful ability to move fluidly in 360 degrees. He often flows inside and outside the court with quickness and grace.

In Spain, many coaches are obsessed with in-and-out movements and defensive movements in particular, which means retreating off the baseline to hit a shot. Toni Nadal and his method stand out because—while Toni does work some defense—the bulk of his training develops forward movement, or "seeking," as Nadal calls it. Nevertheless, great defense is one of the hallmarks of Spanish tennis and, indeed, this book contains a complete chapter dedicated to defense. Curiously, Rafael Nadal demonstrates amazing defensive movement and can retreat off the baseline very well despite Toni's training philosophy on that subject.

Spanish coaches understand that defense starts with great footwork and a willingness to give up ground and move back deeper into the court, away from the baseline. Jose Higueras likes to describe this movement backwards as "absorbing," and he believes in training absorbing with his players. Spanish coaches also spend a lot of time working on the transitions forward and backward from a defensive position to offensive position, "or vice-versa. Pato Alvarez called this the "X" and taught his players to master and "X" movement with double rhythm steps. Bruguera uses a lot of different "X" patterns to train "the give-and-take" on the court. Spanish players learn to move fluidly, not only side to side but forward and back, which aids in their transitional skills.

A selection of classic and modern Spanish footwork drills and complete video reviews and demonstrations are available online. I encourage readers to visit SecretsofSpanishTennis.com or the Chris Lewit YouTube channel to learn more.

The Defensive V

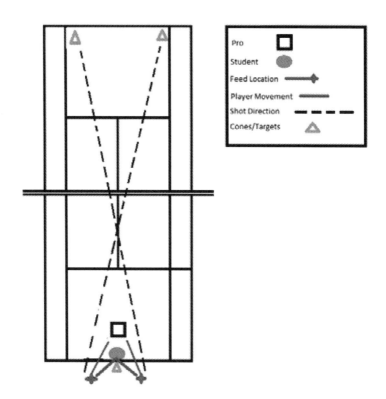

Pro	■
Student	●
Feed Location	�
Player Movement	▬▬▬
Shot Direction	▬ ▬ ▬ ▬
Cones/Targets	▲

Purpose: To train the defensive balance and the stability in the legs using the *doble ritmo* or "double-rhythm" technique of footwork. Getting into position "behind the incoming ball," and effectively loading the body are very important parts of this footwork exercise.

The footwork and balance (feet) can be isolated or the coach can work more holistically on swing shape technique (hands) and tactical (eyes and mind) concurrently

Key Details:

- Wide base and shuffling double rhythm steps; Alvarez discourages crossover steps, but some progressive coaches like Jose Higueras have added crossover steps to the first move. Other more modern coaches allow running steps rather than insisting on the double rhythm as Pato used to do

- Loading on the back leg to promote GRF's (ground reaction forces) but trying not to jump backward unless forced

- Take the ball between hip and shoulder and out in front and a good distance from the trunk. Measuring the contact point well is critical

- The farther back in the court a player defends, the more height and spin the player should apply to the shot

- Hand or racquet fed. Pato also favored racquet taps from the same side of the net. Racquet taps can be downward or upward. Downward taps apply topspin and are for more advanced players (see videos for demonstrations)

Repetitions: 20-60 balls continuously for stamina

Pato Alvarez Attacking V

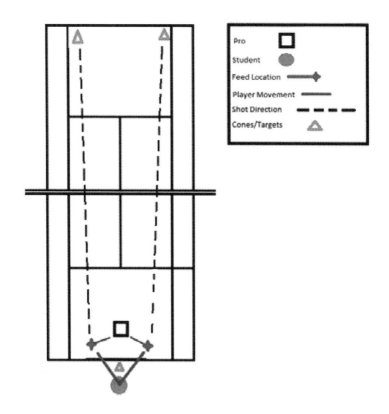

Purpose: To train the offensive balance and the stability in the legs using the "double-rhythm" technique of footwork. Getting into position "behind the incoming ball," and effectively loading the body are very important parts of this footwork exercise. The footwork and balance (feet) can be isolated or the coach can work more holistically on swing shape technique (hands) and tactical (eyes and mind) concurrently

Key Details:

- Moving forward, (Pato emphasized the double-rhythm step) transferring the weight from the back to the front leg during the attack for more linear power. Some modern coaches allow running steps and crossover footwork as well. The running steps are faster than the traditional double rhythm technique which was an obsession for Pato

- It's important to receive the ball between the hips and shoulders and send the ball with racquet speed on a lower trajectory than on the defensive V shots

- On the recovery, Pato preferred the inside pivot and shuffle back to the starting position, often called the "house"—*la casa*. Modern crossover recovery footwork can also be employed

- Positioning behind the ball, taking the ball between the hips and shoulders and out in front, with proper distance from the body, to manage the best contact point possible

- Front foot hop attack move can be encouraged and practiced (see online demonstration)

- Hand or racquet fed. Upward racquet taps from the same side of the net were also favored by Pato on this exercise

Repetitions: 20-60 balls continuously, stamina focused drill

Pato Alvarez Half X Defense and Attack

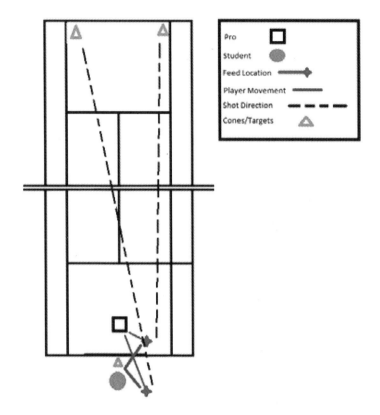

Purpose: To train the defensive and offensive balance, movement and footwork combined. The half X isolates either the forehand or backhand for more focused work rather than alternating forehand and backhand like the V drills

Key Details:

- On the backward movement, the depth, power, and spin of shot is important to make an effective "aggressive defense," a commonly used term in Spain

- Important to load weight onto the back leg to stabilize the body and promote GRF's (ground reaction forces)

- Moving forward, (Pato emphasized the double-rhythm step) transferring the weight from the back to the front leg, when using a closed stance during the attack, for more linear power

- Alternative footwork sequences can be used if the coach or player prefers. For example, the Bruguera method allows for other footwork patterns than exclusively double rhythm. Open to semi-open stance attacks can also be permitted

- Positioning behind the ball, taking the ball with proper distance from the body, between the hips and shoulders and out in front, to manage the best contact point possible

- Hand or racquet fed but upward and downward racquet taps from the same side can also be used. Upward and downward taps will be demonstrated in the drill video

Repetitions: Generally 20 balls or more continuously, stamina focused exercise

Jose Higueras and Jofre Porta Style Drills: Reading, Reaction and Anticipation

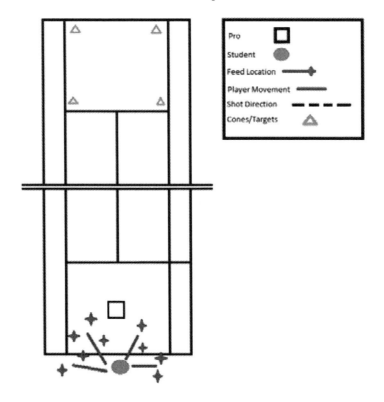

Purpose: To work in primarily an isolated way the eyes (reading), mind (reacting and anticipation), and the feet (footwork, balance and positioning).

Key Details.

- Use quick, random feeds to challenge the player's reading skills and reaction

- The focus should be on quickly getting into position behind the ball with balance and stability and good posture

- The player should focus the eyes on the body language of the coach and the ball release to train tracking (reading skills) and to develop technical anticipation

- Hand fed repetitions: 5-10 balls focusing on short bursts of quickness

Jofre Porta Agility and Quickness Drill Using Resistance Cord

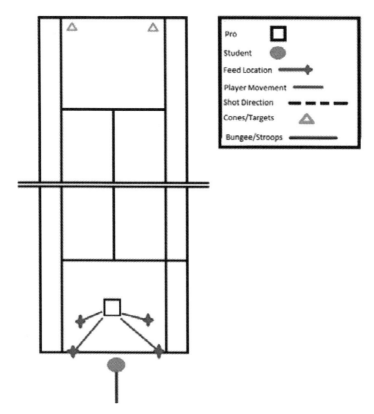

Purpose: To train movement and reaction with quick feeds in many different directions. Jofre likes to add the resistance bungee to further challenge the stability of the player

Key Details:

- The player is strapped into a resistance bungee, typically connected at the waist with a belt

- The feeds from the coach can be lateral and forward into the court

- The coach can isolate one side or alternate toss direction. Focus is on quick movements to the ball

- Maintain balance and stability during the shot execution and keep good posture

- Coach can surprise the player at any time with random tosses

- Generally hand fed

Repetitions: 5-10 balls focusing on balance and short bursts of speed

Bruguera Emergency Movement Drills (with or without use of resistance cord)

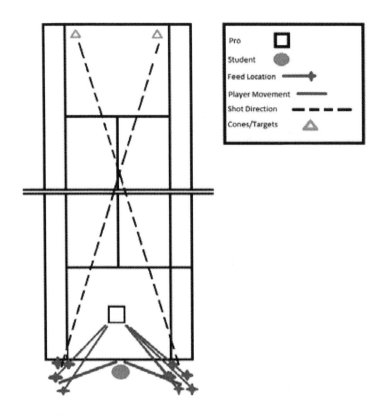

Purpose: To train the emergency defensive lateral movement on the diagonal in a slightly quicker more explosive way. In general, the Spanish believe that players should retreat backward into the court to absorb an attacking shot

Key Details:

- Players are encouraged to work on sliding into this emergency shot when possible

- Coach can isolate either forehand or backhand side, or combine both sides

- The exercise can be patterned or random feeds can be introduced to further challenge the reading, reaction, and anticipation skills

- The player should make a quick and strong recovery after making the shot

- The player should hit defensive topspin shots to the safe zones of the court

- The resistance bungee can be added for additional challenge

- Generally hand fed repetitions: 6-10 repetitions. Hand feeding can go up upward or downward to make more topspin and speed on the ball. (Please see video for demonstration)

Lateral Movement Bruguera Style

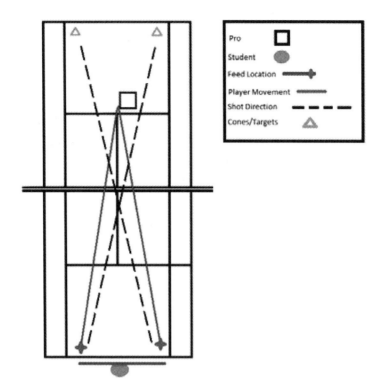

Purpose: To work on running defensive or rally shots under pressure. This exercise trains the player to control his or her body and posture while on the full run in a dangerous situation

Key Details:

- The player must move quickly into position behind the ball managing a good contact point

- Good stability and weight transfer into the shot is important. Maintaining posture in the trunk is key while keeping the head quiet

- Bruguera likes to train a brief or slightly exaggerated pause after the shot to emphasize the importance of stability and body control, then a quick recovery for the next shot is key. For advanced players working at the highest speed, no pause and immediate recovery can be emphasized

- Slide into the shot—not after the shot—to improve movement efficiency and recovery time

- Generally hand fed or racquet fed from across the net to increase realism and ball speed

- Coach can increase tempo to challenge more advanced players

Repetitions: 5-10 to work anaerobically or 20 or more to work more aerobically

Bruguera Classic Reaction Drill

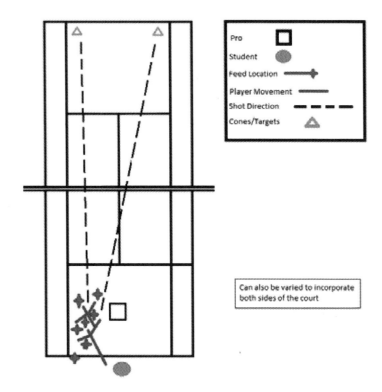

Pro	☐
Student	●
Feed Location	➤
Player Movement	▬▬
Shot Direction	▬ ▬ ▬ ▬
Cones/Targets	△

Can also be varied to incorporate both sides of the court

Purpose: The goal of the exercise is to work on the reading, reaction, and anticipation of the player, and the footwork, balance and positioning. Balance and posture is also stressed throughout the drill.

The drill can also be used more holistically combining technical or tactical awareness and shot selection into the exercise

Key Details:

- The coach tosses random balls forward and backward from the midcourt

- The player must read the situation, react quickly to the incoming ball, and position himself with balance and stability, receiving the ball with a good contact point

- The player should be encouraged to track and read the coach's body language and to anticipate the next random toss

- Hand fed

Repetitions: 10-20 depending on how much suffering desired

Toni Nadal Box Seeking Drill

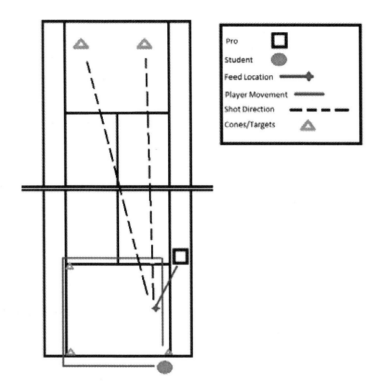

Purpose: A Toni Nadal favorite for beginning players to work on a fundamental footwork patterns and seeking the ball by going forward to receive it

Key Details:

- The coach hand tosses one ball from a fixed position. However, the coach can sometimes toss the ball forward a short distance to challenge the forward movement and positioning of the player

- After hitting the ball, the player moves along the box, shuffling along the lateral sides of the box, drawn with cones, backpedaling along the opposite side to where the coach stands, shuffling across to another cone, and then running forward on the coach's side to hit another the hand tossed ball

- Toni always favors using cones for targets on the other side of the net

- The coach is positioned very close to the player when the player strikes the ball and this can facilitate good communication and makes it easy for the coach to fine tune the technique by making adjustments with his hands

- Toni always asks for "una pausa," a short pause after each stroke so that he can check the posture and balance

- Toni is obsessed with the extension or *accompaniment* of the ball as well as lifting the ball to pass over the net with good margin

- Hand tossed gently

Repetitions: Typically 10-15 balls. Coach's preference

Toni Nadal Lateral Ladder Drill

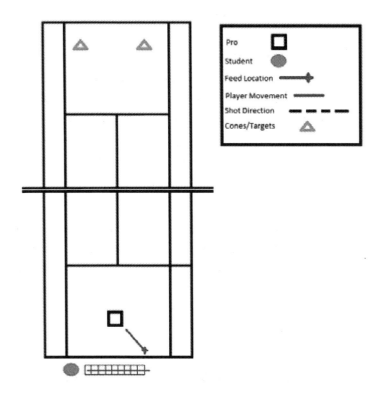

Purpose: Toni Nadal often likes to employ the agility ladder during on court exercises to give additional footwork challenges to his students. Nadal has many ladder drills that he likes. In this particular exercise, the ladder is set up laterally behind the baseline. Players work on different footwork agility patterns across the ladder while also tracking the coach to anticipate a hand fed short ball. The combination of agility and footwork, along with reading and anticipating with the eyes, make for an excellent comprehensive movement exercise

Key Details:

- Agility ladder is placed laterally near baseline

- The player performs a coach prescribed agility footwork pattern on the ladder and when reaching the end of the ladder the coach tosses one ball to the forehand. Then the player moves the opposite direction along the ladder to hit one backhand. The coach can also toss random short balls to challenge the reaction of the player as described below

- Toni usually stresses closed stance, balance and body control when receiving the ball. Toni allows for open stances and controlled jumping for more advanced players

- Hand fed

- The coach can randomize the timing of the toss to train the eyes, mind, and feet of the player. In this variation, the player will perform the prescribed footwork pattern back and forth along the ladder, and then the coach will toss the ball at some point while the player is still on the ladder rather than always coordinating the toss when the player reaches the end of the ladder

- When performed intensely, this exercise carries a high neural demand and can be physically exhausting

Repetitions: Can be anywhere from 6 to 15 or more repetitions depending on the level, or players can rotate, alternating with others in the group

Toni Nadal Drive Invertido Drill

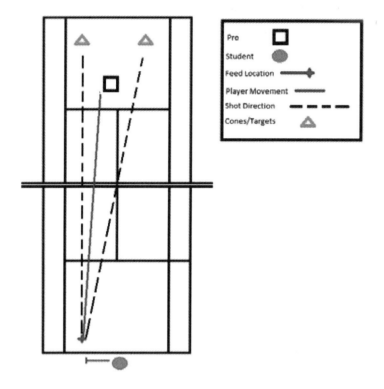

Purpose: The goal of the exercise is to work the quick movement of the feet around a ball coming to the backhand corner in order to set up and hit a forehand. Toni's objective is to develop the reading of the eyes and the coordination of feet by challenging the player with an inverted movement. The player must arrive to hit the ball with good balance and posture. *Invertido* means *inverted* and *drive* means *forehand* in Spanish; therefore the "drive invertido" is commonly known as the inside-out or inside-in forehand in the US. Toni likes to train inverted shots to challenge the eyes, balance, and body orientation of a player. Interestingly, Pato Álvarez also has a number of drills like this in his repertoire including inverted *backhand* footwork drills. Amazingly, Jofre Porta will even actually spin his players around 360 degrees in between shots to challenge their balance! Inverted hitting is a common theme in Spanish footwork training!

Key Details:

- The coach sends a ball to the backhand corner. The player must run around the ball, set up, and hit an inside-out or inside-in forehand

- The drill can be all inside outs, all inside ins, alternating, or any pattern the coach would like

- Toni usually stresses balance, body control, and stability in this exercise

- The distance measurement and spacing between body and ball is paramount when inverting

- The player should position with a good base of support and should explode off the ground, rotate in the air, and land with stability and width

- Hand fed or racquet fed

Repetitions: Toni typically works in repetition ranges of 8-15 balls, but the coach can do more if more suffering is desired

Toni Nadal Half X Drill

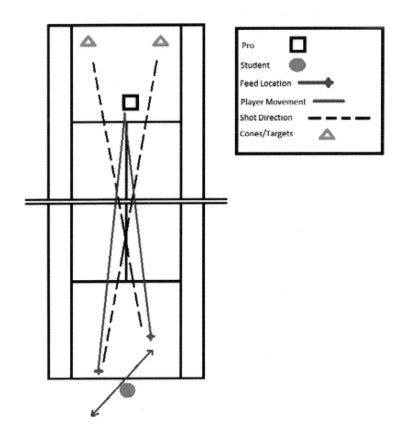

Purpose: When Toni does his X drill variations the focus is on the positioning, the tactical orientation, and decision making above all else. Making the best possible shot from the defense and being aggressive and powerful on the offense is key. Toni uses this half X drill to work on the transition from defense to offense and to develop a good attack

Key Details:

- Toni allows for whatever footwork pattern the player finds comfortable within the certain parameters he sets. He is not rigid in his application of movement the way Pato tended to be

- Take the ball between hips and   out in front, and a good distance from the trunk—measuring the contact point well is critical

- The farther back a player defends, the more height and spin the player should apply to the shot. Toni wants very aggressive attack shots on the shorter balls

- Players can jump and use open stances on the forehands, and are especially encouraged to do so on the attack forehands

- Nadal prefers racquet feeding from across the net. Toni also like to feed advanced players with a slight topspin on his ball as opposed to Bruguera who typically feeds a flatter ball, for example

- Sometimes Toni will overweight the attack shots by giving two forehand attacks consecutively for every one defensive backhand

- The drill can also be performed all forehands with an inverted defensive or offensive forehand, which is a cool variation! Check video demonstrations at the book website or the Chris Lewit YouTube channel

Repetitions: Toni typically favors moderate repetition ranges from 6-15 balls

Toni Nadal 2 V 1 Wall

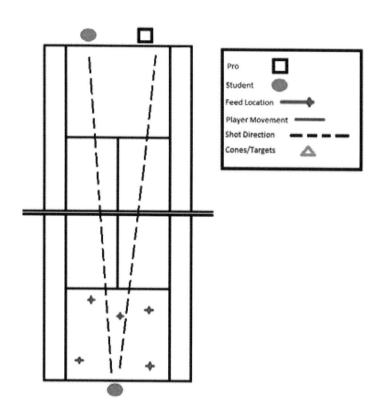

Purpose: To develop good movements both vertical and horizontally on the court while developing consistency and control of the ball. Toni loves to do this drill with two players

Key Details:

- The coach becomes *la pared*, "the wall" in Spanish. In this case, the coach makes the wall from the baseline and chips the ball back to the solo player

- The coach should chip the ball softly with height to allow the player time to adjust and operate the feet well. The coach can vary the chip short and deep, and wide to challenge the player's movement

- The player should maintain good spacing, posture and balance, and contact point management throughout while reading the incoming ball

- The player on the coaches side, the wall side, should play normal topspin balls and move the solo player around the court. In this way, the solo player can work on receiving more difficult topspin balls and easier balls chipped by the coach

- Many different patterns can be used but Toni likes the basic pattern of two balls hit to the player on the same side as the coach and then one ball to the coach, for example

- The entire exercise can also be performed by the player with all forehand and inverted forehands—no backhands—which is very footwork intensive and tiring

- Some coaches like to call "play the point" or "go to net" after a good rally to add a fun element to the exercise after the player demonstrates hard work

Repetitions: Toni doesn't do this drill with a fixed number in mind, but he typically wants a good rhythm and control demonstrated. The solo player typically works for a few minutes trying to achieve good control and footwork and then the players will switch places. It's possible to use just one or two balls for several minutes if the players are focused and steady

Toni Nadal Eyes and Reaction

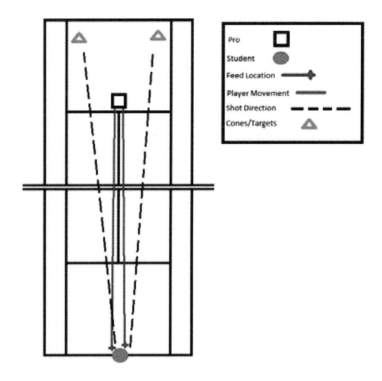

Purpose: Toni says this exercise can help a player develop their eye tracking, the reactions in the nervous system, and to learn how to manage fast incoming balls. Training the eyes and reaction is popular in Spain especially in the Bruguera system as well. Moreover, this exercise develops critical on-the-rise skills and teaches the player how to take the ball early, which are subjects not traditionally emphasized in Spain

Key Details:

- The player is positioned near the center mark near the baseline or just inside the baseline

- The coach is positioned near the opposite service T and sends balls at a high speed in rapid succession straight up the middle at the player

- The priorities for the player are eyes tracking early and quick reaction, quick turn and shortening backswing, and making small quick footwork adjustments to the incoming flight of the ball

- Toni always stresses balance, body control, and stability, and in this drill the player also has to drop his or her base of support and get very low with the legs without losing erect posture in the trunk

- Toni believes in a more aggressive court position and taking the ball early more than most coaches in Spain. Many younger, more progressive coaches are also starting to train their players to take the ball earlier so that they can be stronger on hard courts. The work of the team at Ferrero Tennis Academy is a great example of this trend as demonstrated by the way Carlos Alcaraz—who trained at the academy since 15 years old—plays

- The player should stay relatively low through the shot rather than jumping up

- Racquet fed with pace

- There is another variation of this drill that Toni likes where the feeds can be anywhere, which really makes the player suffer. That drill will be discussed in Chapter 6

Repetitions: Can be anywhere from 8 to 20 repetitions

Pato Alvarez Inverted Movements

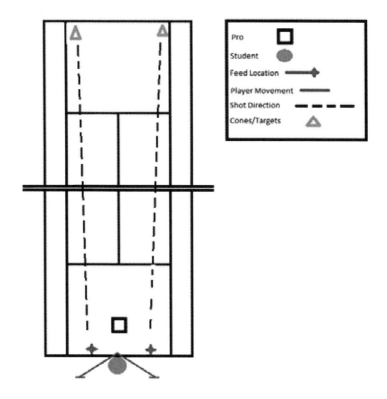

Purpose: A famous Pato drill where the player must invert both on the forehand and backhand side from the baseline. The drill develops the eyes and footwork, especially spacing, balance and body orientation to the incoming ball

Key Details:

- The player moves side to side or in a V pattern along the baseline

- Player should take the ball between hips and out in front, and a good distance from the trunk. Measuring the contact point well is critical

- The balance is crucial and the player must maintain erect posture throughout the swing and movements

- Pato classically preferred the closed stance and moving with the double rhythm steps but the drill can be adapted to allow a variety of movement patterns and stances

- The coach hand feeds or gently taps the ball upward with the racquet

- The coach is positioned on the same side of the court as the player

Repetitions: 20-40 balls but Pato's drills could sometimes go longer—much longer!

Jofre Porta's Spin Drill

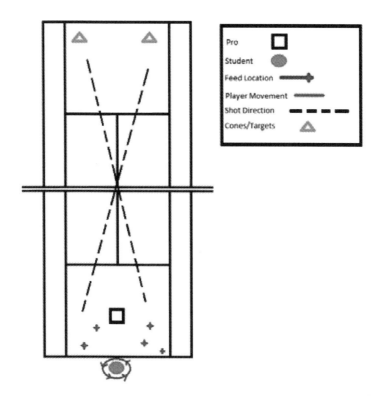

Purpose: A unique footwork and movement drill from the genius mind of Jofre Porta. The exercise uses a 360 degree spin to disorient the player and challenge the balance and spacing from the incoming ball

Key Details:

- The player hits a shot from the baseline and, after recovering back to the middle, spins around 360 degrees

- The player must work hard to maintain balance, body control, and good posture at all times

- The coach feeds balls left and right along the baseline or can randomize the feeds

- Jofre often hand feeds the balls while standing on the same side of the net as the player

- The spin move can also be combined with inverted footwork for additional challenge

Repetitions: Jofre typically feeds 8-12 balls

The above drills will dramatically improve reaction, ball tracking, multidirectional movement skills, and balance. The Spanish approach to working on footwork is the best in the world. Coaches, parents, and players can learn a lot from the Spanish way and can incorporate the Spanish exercises shown here into their training programs in a general way, or specifically tailor the exercises depending on the player's needs.

Additional free high quality footwork videos can be found on the book website (SecretsofSpanishTennis.com) or on the Chris Lewit YouTube channel. I have also developed a wonderful and comprehensive footwork course called #Flow at the CLTA online school (CLTA.teachable.com).

CHAPTER 2

Building The Heavy Ball: Weapon And Racquet Speed Development

"I think acceleration is the most important thing. You can play with timing and this and that, but in the end, the ball has to run, has to go fast"
—*Albert Costa, 2002 French Open champion*

Sergi Bruguera changed the Spanish game with his impressive racquet speed and powerful heavy topspin forehand. His father and coach, Lluis has said, "It changed a lot with Sergi. I changed completely the style of practice, and how we can play." He asked himself, "How, without power, the ball of Sergi and the ball of the Spanish players can go faster...Not with power in the body or the arm, but with the racquet?" Bruguera developed drills to try and train his players to develop racquet speed like his son Sergi. Rafael Nadal's forehand was built in exactly the same mold as Sergi's—undoubtedly influenced heavily by the Bruguera method of acceleration training. Lluis Bruguera was a visionary, and in the 1980s he modeled his players after Bjorn Borg, anticipating (and simultaneously hastening) the trend of modern tennis with its emphasis on power and spin. He trained his players to develop maximum RPM on the forehand and he created drills to develop racquet speed like his protege, Jordi Arrese (former ATP No. 23 and silver medalist at the 1992 Olympics) and his son Sergi. Nadal was the first modern player to surpass Sergi's RPM spin rate on the forehand, and it is shocking to realize how much RPM Sergi had in the 1980s and early 90s with less advanced racquet technology and without the use of high-tech poly strings!

It seems that almost all Spanish coaches—to some extent—are obsessed with racquet speed and developing a powerful, heavy topspin forehand. The Spanish method of developing the heavy ball—in particular, the big, heavy forehand—is truly unique and remarkable in the tennis training world. All coaches, players and parents can learn a tremendous amount about how to build big, heavy groundstrokes from the Spanish system.

Over the years, I have written extensively about how Spanish coaches develop the forehand for many publications, and especially for John Yandell's Tennisplayer magazine (Tennisplayer.net). While the technique of the forehand is not the purview of this chapter, any reader who is curious about more technical details of the Spanish forehand, please feel free to search for the article "Building the Spanish Style Forehand."

There are also many free videos on the Spanish forehand on the Chris Lewit YouTube channel as well and a complete development course called #Whip at the CLTA online school (CLTA.teachable.com).

First and foremost, the best asset the Spanish have to help develop heavy balls is the slow, red, European clay. If you have never played on clay in Spain, the courts are *very* slow and they force the player to swing fast to send the ball over the net, deep into the court. Also, the balls get a lot of moisture on them and clay builds up on them—making them literally heavier— and this forces the player to swing faster than on hard courts to send that heavy ball across the net.

The clay courts are the second teacher, helping to train players about the need for racquet speed. Because taking the ball on the rise is not a consistently viable option on clay (due to bad bounces), players typically hit the ball at the top of the bounce or let the ball fall into their strike zone (losing energy all the way), thus they must generate their own pace rather than using the energy of the ball by taking it on the rise.

Thus the clay is a big help to the Spanish coach, assisting him in building efficient acceleration on groundstrokes. This is another reason why the clay courts in Spain are considered the second teacher. But this is just where it begins in Spain... In addition to the inherent benefits of the slow red clay courts, the Spanish have developed a great system of drills to develop the whip and acceleration of the shot. Bruguera said that the "racquet must make more speed, like a lasso that is moving very fast..." All the classic Bruguera drills, "from the basket, with the hand, and with the volley" work on the fundamental skill of racquet speed. "I tried to imagine how my players can make more speed in the racquet without power (being physically strong)," he said. "Within the power of the opponent...the wrist, the racquet, the arm, and the transfer of the body: that gives to you a lot more power than anything else."

Bruguera's ingenious system of drills for racquet acceleration have trickled down to the armada of coaches in Spain from the next generations. These coaches have taken his drills, adapted and modified them, and proliferated them at nearly every school all across the country. In addition, the RFET, The Royal Spanish Tennis Federation, also invited Lluis to many conferences and workshops to share his new method. In this way, the philosophy and drills of Lluis Bruguera became part of the curriculum for coaches seeking to get certified in Spain and became part of the fabric of the coaching culture in the country.

When the drills, the surface, and the constant reminders to students to swing fast and develop a weapon are all integrated, the result is a system that synergistically and consistently produces players who hit big and heavy groundstrokes. The heavy ball in Spain is not just an accident or due to a player's DNA, it is actively and systematically developed.

I believe other countries could adopt the same philosophy and the drills of the Spanish coaches to help their players hit heavier, which is one of the keys to success on the modern professional tour. Indeed, over the past decade or so, many countries have started to do just that: integrating Spanish techniques and methods into their coaching curriculums and hiring away Spanish coaches to mentor and train coaches.

Even without red clay, the heavy ball can be developed if properly nourished with the right drills and reminders. Of course the clay helps. A heavy ball is a shot that is deep and penetrating, with power AND spin—not just pace. The weight of the shot comes from the spin component added to power and depth. Sometimes players from other countries hit big groundstrokes, but they are often flatter, with less margin for error, and the shots don't jump off the courts with as much heaviness from topspin. What player wouldn't want more spin for consistency and the ability to hit better angles without sacrificing power? The Sampras forehand was great, for example, but Spanish coaches would argue that Rafa's forehand is better and more versatile, with the ability to dominate on all surfaces.

An entire chapter in this book could be dedicated to the Big Spanish Forehand. In Spain, the big Alcaraz, Nadal or Moya style forehand is also an obsession. Players are taught to consistently run around their backhand, even if the backhand is good, to rip the big forehand. This is because physiologically and biomechanically, the forehand can generate more power and spin, which is necessary to win on clay (but is also useful on other surfaces).

Indeed, most elite coaches agree that players who train on clay find it easier to transition to hard courts than the other way around. Many top coaches believe this, including Jose Higueras. Said Sergio Casal of Spanish tennis, "The guys here, they all play on clay. Even without a system, you get strong, you get consistent. I think it's very important to start here to play."

One explanation is that a big heavy forehand or backhand is an asset no matter who you are playing or what the surface is—a sentiment that I agree with. If a player grows up on a fast court and never learns to accelerate, always receiving help from the surface speed, this player will struggle mightily trying to transition to slow clay court tennis. A good clay court forehand will work on hard courts, but a good hard court forehand may not work well on clay. Rafa's forehand is big no matter what. Who wouldn't trade in their stroke for the forehand of Alcaraz? Would anyone say these forehands are only good on clay? No. These types of Spanish forehands are versatile, not clay court dependent; they are just great big shots—period.

Drills To Develop Weapons and Racquet Speed

Complete video reviews and demonstrations are available online. I encourage readers to visit www. SecretsofSpanishTennis. com and the Chris Lewit YouTube page for more complete explanations of the nuances of the following exercises and to visually see me demonstrating the drills with my students.

The Classic Swinging Volley Drill

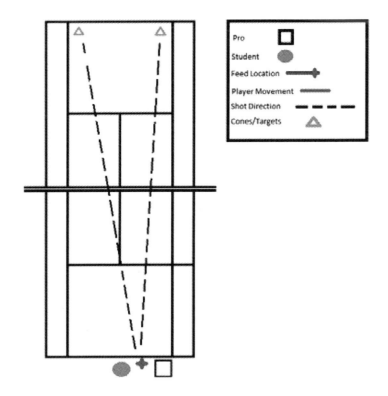

Purpose: Probably the most famous exercise from Spain developed by Lluis Bruguera; it has been adopted by many coaches around the world, and variations are used all over Spain. The purpose of the exercise is to train the arm and racquet acceleration to deliver a strong, deep, and heavy ball that combines spin with pace. A secondary benefit is to develop the timing for the swing volley

Key Details:

- Player hits swinging volleys rapidly in succession from baseline focusing on creating a deep, heavy spin, power shot

- Coach hand tosses the balls from the side. Sometimes the coach can feed from the front but it's safer for the coach to feed from the side

- The player's arm should be relatively relaxed to get more whip

- Bruguera classically strongly emphasizes a closed stance and a focus on arm speed rather than open stance loading although some Spanish coaches do allow semi and open stances in this type of drill

- Proper loading and weight transfer to the front leg is key if the player is using a closed stance

- Good balance and relatively still upper body and head position are essential as the arm whips through the contact zone

Repetitions: Generally 8-12

Bruguera Racquet Speed Drill

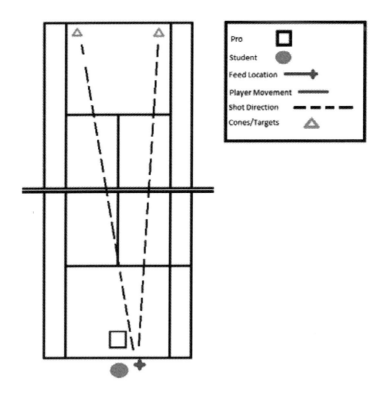

Purpose: Same purpose as the previous exercise, but with the ball hit off the bounce, to develop the elusive Spanish "heavy ball"—big time acceleration. This exercise also improves the reading skills (eyes) and the quick reaction and preparation of the body, as the ball comes at a fast tempo

Key Details:

- The player hits groundstrokes rapidly in succession from baseline focusing on creating a deep, heavy spin, power shot

- Coach hand tosses the ball from the front at a safe angle and increases the tempo of tosses to overload the player's arm

- Arm(s) should be relatively relaxed to get more whip

- Bruguera classically strongly emphasizes a closed stance and a focus on arm speed rather than open stance loading, although other coaches in Spain allow semi-open and open stances

- Proper loading and weight transfer to the front leg

- Good balance and relatively still upper body as arm whips through the contact zone

Repetitions: Generally 10-20

Aggressive Defense Heavy Ball

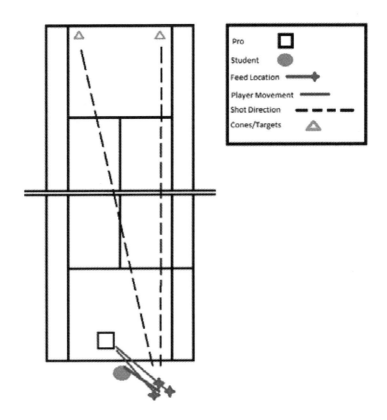

Pro	☐
Student	●
Feed Location	➡
Player Movement	━━━
Shot Direction	▬ ▬ ▬ ▬
Cones/Targets	△

Purpose: This exercise is used to develop the movement and racquet acceleration necessary to hit an aggressive heavy defense, or an attacking high bouncing shot from deeper in the court. The player is pushed back deep behind the baseline to practice the aggressive defense

Key Details:

- The player should load the back leg using good ground reaction forces GRFs

- Arm should be relatively relaxed to get more whip

- Pato and Lluis have favored the closed stance and would advise proper loading and weight transfer to the front leg, and to avoid the open stance and falling backward when possible. Some next generation Spanish coaches allow semi-open and open stances and fading away from the shot

- The player should demonstrate good balance and a relatively still upper body and head position as the racquet whips through the contact zone

- Moderate tempo and high tosses from the coach are key to give player time to adjust position before loading and accelerating

- Hand or racquet fed

Repetitions: 10-20

Bruguera Tempo Swinging Volleys

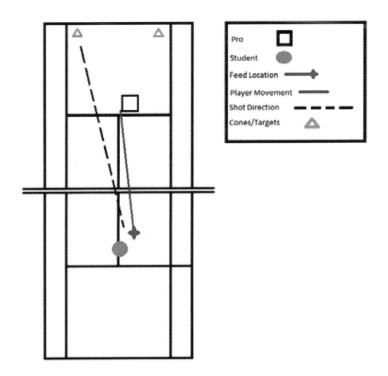

Purpose: Another famous Bruguera exercise to develop the racquet acceleration. This exercise also improves the reading skills (eyes) and the quick reaction and preparation of the body, as the ball comes at a fast tempo. This drill works the swinging volley attack from the midcourt area, which is important tactically, especially on clay; however, the primary purpose is to physically overload the arm to develop more acceleration. The coach, however, can vary the teaching emphasis and make the drill more tactically and pattern oriented or holistic, rather than technical, if desired

Key Details:

- Player hits successive swinging volleys at a rapid tempo, which serves to overload the arm

- Footwork and adjustments are important to manage the contact point

- Player should keep upper body relatively quiet, head still, and "pass the arm and racquet quickly," as coaches commonly say in Spain, through the hitting zone as fast as possible

- Bruguera prefers that players use the neutral stance.

- Racquet fed

Repetitions: 8-12

The Alvarez and Druguera "Wall"—

La Pared—All Forehand or

All Backhand Focus

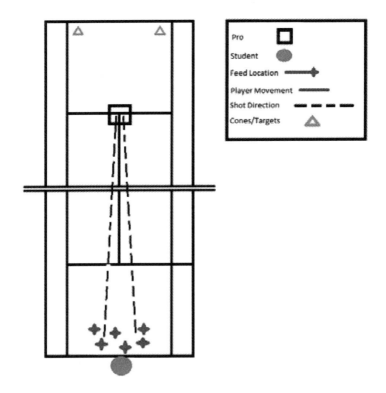

Purpose: Another very famous exercise seen all over Spain in many different variations is *la pared*, or wall drill. The primary purpose, when isolating one side, is to overload the arm(s) and legs to develop more strength, power, and racquet speed acceleration, although the exercise is very versatile and can be used to train other areas and also can be certainly used for more holistic training and tactical training as well. I will discuss other variations in later chapters

Key Details:

- The coach is at the net and volleys softly, lofting the ball to the player. The player must adjust feet and hit a heavy ball to the coach's chest or another target the coach designates

- It is important for the coach to be like a wall, never missing the volley, and consistently putting the ball softly back to the player; thus the drill does require a high level of volley skill

- It is important for the player to focus on loading the legs well, making the perfect contact point, and accelerating as much as possible, hitting the heavy ball with power and spin

- A great and popular variation is for the coach to shout "now" from time to time, indicating that the player should hit a clean winner to another target on the court away from the coach. This variation is a great way to train the decisive forehand kill shot

- The closer the coach stands to the net, the less time the player has and the more intense the exercise gets. Top Spanish coach Francis Roig, Rafa's travel coach, likes to employ this variation

Repetitions: 10 to 20 or more or for time (2 or 3 minutes for example)

Higueras Low Whip and High Whip

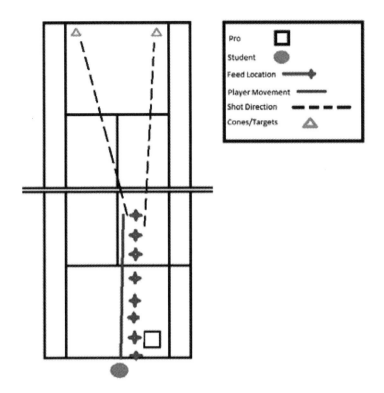

Purpose: This is one of the drills Jose Higueras implemented in the USTA Player Development system when he was director of coaching. The exercise is used for developing racquet speed and a flexible wrist/forearm movement on lower contact point balls. This drill is rumored to have been one of Rafa Nadal's favorites when he was a kid

Key Details:

- The coach faces the player and hand feeds the balls in rapid succession from a safe angle while back peddling towards the net from the baseline

- The player has to adjust positioning and lower body to make a better contact point, and he or she must apply spin to the ball to safely clear the net

- Acceleration and good body stability should be stressed. The head should be still

- As the feeds get closer and closer to the net, the player will have to use more forearm/wrist lift and spin

- Coach can vary high and low hand feeds or randomize the tosses for extra challenge

Repetitions: 8-10

Toni Nadal Inverted
Velocidad y Habilidad

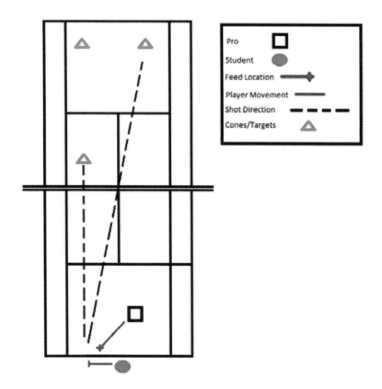

Purpose: One of my favorite weapon building Toni Nadal drills, Velocity and Touch, develops the power forehand and complements that shot with the development of a soft drop shot. Carlos Alcaraz demonstrates great acceleration on his forehand but also great feel on the dropshot. This exercise develops both qualities. Inverted, or *invertido*, simply means

111

the player hits the forehand from the backhand corner of the court, running around the backhand

Key Details:

- The coach feeds the player an inverted forehand (*drive invertido*) two times in succession. The first ball the player rips with power and spin, and the second ball the player feathers a drop shot

- The player must achieve a good inverted position with balance, and explode up into the power shot. The player must disguise the drop shot well by faking a power topspin forehand

- Acceleration on the power shot and soft touch on the drop shot should be stressed by the coach

- The coach can create variations like both shots need to be to the same side targets, alternating direction targets, or the coach can add any other parameters to vary the exercise

- Racquet fed with the coach positioned across the net. The ball to be ripped is fed softly—floated with loft—so that the player must generate all the power

Repetitions: 8-16 repetitions

Toni Nadal Shot Velocity Live Ball Drill

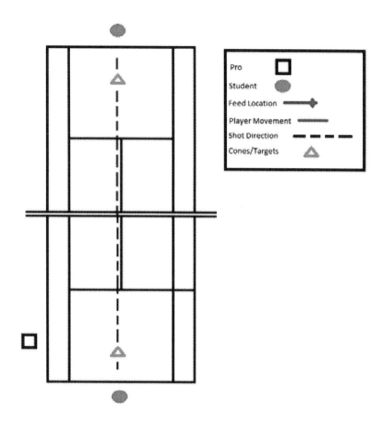

Purpose: A wonderful live ball exercise—one of many from the mind of Uncle Toni. This drill features two players rallying down the middle of the court with one player defending and the other player steadily increasing the pace of his or her shots. Thus the power player learns to incrementally hit with more power without losing too much body or ball control. The goal is power —but with control and consistency

Key Details:

- All shots from both players stay in the middle of the court to help prolong the rally. No winners to the side

- The player who is changing speeds with power must steadily increase his or her racquet speed. The defending player must retrieve every ball and play at the same steady velocity

- After a set amount of time or repetitions the players should switch roles with the power player becoming the defender and vice-versa

- Another variation for advanced players—they can start slow together and build power together incrementally until control is lost

- Live ball rally exercise

Repetitions: 10-30 power shots then switch roles or change roles based on time (e.g. one or two minutes)

Toni Nadal Three Forehand Attacks

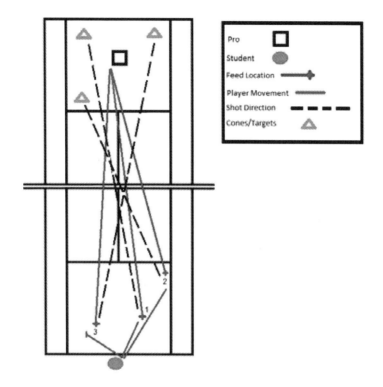

Purpose: To develop a versatile and powerful topspin forehand that can be used to attack three different ways. Toni believes in a powerful and aggressive attack game built around a devastating forehand weapon

Key Details:

- The coach feeds the player three different situations in succession. The first situation is a strong, deep crosscourt forehand attack. The second feed is for a sharp angle forehand attack. The third situation is an inverted forehand attack inside-out

- Another good variation is the first feed for an inside-out forehand. The second feed for the deep crosscourt attack. And the third feed is for the sharp angle

- The player should work hard to get in the best possible position with the legs and accelerate fully on the shots

- It's important for the player to keep a stable head and upright trunk during the shot

Repetitions: Can be anywhere from 9-15 repetitions

Toni Nadal Inverted Attack

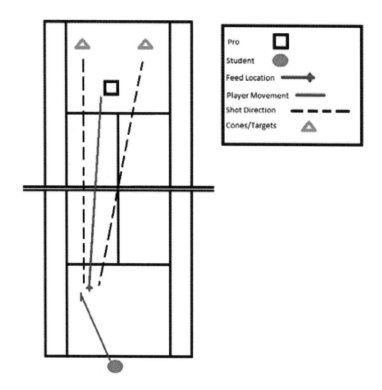

Purpose: The goal of the exercise is to work the quick movement of the feet around a ball coming to the backhand corner in order to set up and hit a forehand. Toni's objective is to develop the reading of the eyes and the coordination of feet by challenging the player with an inverted movement. The player must arrive to hit the ball with good balance and posture

Key Details:

- Toni likes to frequently train inverted shots to challenge the eyes, balance, and body orientation of a player. Interestingly, Pato Álvarez also has a number of drills like this in his repertoire including inverted *backhand* footwork drills. Amazingly, Jofre Porta will even actually spin his players around 360 degrees in between shots to challenge their balance! One of Jofre's spin drills is featured in Chapter 1. Inverted hitting is a common theme in Spanish footwork training

- The coach sends a ball to the backhand corner. The player must run around the ball, set up, and hit an inside out or inside in forehand with maximum acceleration

- The drill can be all inside outs, all inside ins, alternating, with different targets in any pattern the coach would like

- Toni usually stresses balance, body control, stability, and acceleration in this exercise

- The player should position with a good base of support and should explode off the ground, rotate in the air, and land with stability and width. Toni encourages his students to jump on the forehand shot

- Hand fed or racquet fed

Repetitions: Can be anywhere from 8 to 15 repetitions

Other Helpful Supplementary Weapon Building Methods Commonly Seen In Spain:

- Wind exercises (rapid shadow swings). See demonstration in the Secrets of Spanish Tennis video collection at SecretsofSpanishTennis.com or the Chris Lewit YouTube channel

- Medicine ball work. Medicine ball throws to simulate forehands and backhands are very popular in Spain

- Resistance band training. The resistance bands can be used for acceleration training on the groundstrokes

- Any pulley or cable devices such as the Versa Pulley are great exercises to build power in the groundstrokes

Please visit www.SecretsofSpanishTennis.com and the Chris Lewit YouTube channel for video guides to these supplementary exercises.

Specific, systematic training of the racquet acceleration is perhaps the most important part of the Spanish contribution to modern tennis training, and much of the credit has to go to Lluis Bruguera, the visionary who designed many of the famous Spanish racquet speed drills.

All parents, coaches, and players should understand the importance of acceleration training to reaching the highest possible level in tennis and maximizing player potential. Too many players underachieve because their rally ball does not have enough speed and they never develop enough acceleration to have a world-class weapon. In fact, I would argue that this is one of the biggest coaching myths still prevalent, especially in the US, in modern tennis teaching: that acceleration cannot and should not be taught.

The Spanish have developed the best system on the planet for training power and racquet acceleration to get that modern heavy, power topspin ball, especially on the forehand side. There is no doubt that acceleration training and weapon building has been a significant contributor to the success of Spanish players and Spain's rise to the top of world tennis.

Consider adding racquet speed training to your existing regime. One of the beautiful elements of Spanish racquet speed training is that the exercises are modular and flexible. The simplicity and versatility of the exercises allows them to be interwoven into any training system or successfully adapted for specific individual needs.

CHAPTER 3

Patience and Consistency

"To be solid, to make no mistakes on the court, this quells anxiety and brings confidence."
—Lluis Bruguera

"The game of tennis, at its essence, is still a game of errors"
—William "Pato" Alvarez

Spanish players have always been known for being solid from the backcourt. Even since the days of the slice backhand and flat forehand in the 1960s and 1970s, Spanish players did not miss very often and did not give away many free points with unforced errors. Today the modern Spanish players hit harder and with more topspin, but they still carry on the original Spanish philosophy: that the game of tennis is essentially won and lost by the amount of errors made, not winners.

This fundamental concept is part of the fabric of the coaching and playing culture in Spain—it permeates every drill and every on-court training session. Young players are taught to be patient, to learn to build points, and win through attrition rather than to go for broke early.

The red clay helps, of course, by slowing down the speed of the ball and allowing players to run down more shots. The clay reinforces the virtues of patience, control, and consistency that are so often preached by the coaches.

One of the classic hallmarks of Spanish players is a very high shot tolerance, a term coined by Eliot Teltscher (former top 10 player from the United States and now a high performance coach) to describe a player's level of patience and consistency.

What I realized as I began to study with leading Spanish coaches, like Bruguera and Alvarez, and after visiting the leading academies in Spain, was that shot tolerance was being taught not just by the clay but by the teaching methods of both the coaches and schools. Patience and consistency are not just traits that naturally develop in players in Spain; rather, they are also actively and systematically taught.

The drilling system developed by Lluis Bruguera and Pato Alvarez in the 1970s and 1980s, which emphasizes both consistency and concentration, seems to have infiltrated every coach's handbook, and the basic Spanish consistency drills are ubiquitously found at every program that I have visited across the country. (These drills will be discussed more specifically and demonstrated at the end of this chapter.)

Essentially, young kids in Spain are drilled relentlessly from a young age to never miss, and to have more shot tolerance and discipline than the guy across the net. Then they go and play the majority of their practice matches and tournaments—week in and week out—on the slow red clay, which further reinforces the value of patience.

This mentality may change in the coming decades as Spanish coaches reinvent themselves and Spanish academies continue to install more and more hard courts in an effort to create more well-rounded players who can attack more. Indeed, Carlos Alcaraz exemplifies a new more aggressive mold of Spanish player.

In the 1960s and 70s, the Spanish ethos of never missing was derided as too defensive or conservative, and many coaches still make the same critique today. Spanish players are still often mocked as "pushers" by coaches and players from other countries.

As I have tried to explain in the previous chapter, in the last 20 to 30 years, the Spanish have become obsessed with developing power and racquet speed on the groundstrokes. Anyone who refers to modern Spanish players as "pushers" is either ignorant or misinformed. Yes, the Spanish do value consistency and patience over winners and hyper aggressiveness, but the Spanish fundamentally teach consistency with aggressive racquet speed, which is something very different than pushing. Pushers tend to decelerate the racquet through the hitting zone.

Pushers tend to send the ball high and down the middle with little tactical game plan other than to wait and react. The modern Spanish method to develop the baseline game couldn't be more diametrically opposed to this approach.

In Spain, the coaches preach consistency but ALWAYS with big acceleration. The coaches preach the doctrine of no mistakes, but aggressive ball control, using heavy groundstrokes to pin the opponent to the baseline and move them around the court to make them run and tire out.

Most Spanish academies are also practicing a lot on hard courts to develop all surface players who can attack when necessary. Said Albert Costa, "All the juniors are practicing in hard courts. The precision that we [work on], we do it half in clay courts and half in hard courts. We know that it's important to develop the tennis in hard courts... I want to have complete players. Not just clay court players."

The modern Spanish game delivers big forehands and crushing backhands—winners—when the time is right. The difference is that the Spanish players know they can grind if they have to. They know they can hit 20 groundstrokes in a row if necessary and the situation warrants that strategy. Spanish players have a Plan B if the winners aren't going in on that particular day. All players growing up in Spain develop the confidence from the baseline that comes from developing patience and consistency with acceleration, not by pushing. Carlos Alcaraz, Rafael Nadal, Alejandro Davidovich Fokina, Carlos Moya, David Ferrer, and Fernando Verdasco are good examples of modern day players with great baseline consistency and the explosive ability to hit big winners after building points. These are prototypical of the kind of players that are being built in Spain today.

The Three C's

The Spanish work very hard to develop what I call the three C's: Control, Consistency, and Concentration. Bruguera emphasizes, "To be solid, to be consistent is not to be a defensive player." He argues that, "The confidence comes when you know you can do it without missing...If I am consistent. If I know I can do it. Minimum? I don't lose." Consistency breeds confidence.

One of the most powerful and classic Spanish ways to develop consistency, control, concentration, and of course patience, is by extending drills way beyond the normal amount of repetitions coaches might use in the United States. If the typical U.S. coach feeds one, two or three shots, the typical Spanish coach feeds 10, 20, or 30 or more shots in one exercise without a break or rest. Some of the younger coaching generations will feed in a lower repetition range of 8-15 balls, but the older guard like Pato and Lluis like to do long sets with many repetitions.

It's also important to mention that in Spain, the typical student-to-court ratio is two or three kids maximum, generally two kids per court, as opposed to four to six kids per court at the typical American camp or academy. All across Spain at top academies the ratio tends to be two kids per court—or the occasional max of three. The Spanish believe that two kids per court is essential to giving advanced players high quality training. The systems as designed by Lluis and Pato just wouldn't work with four or more kids per court because the idea is to give each player long sets of 20 or more repetitions per set. There would just be too much waiting around if Spanish coaches drilled this way with four or more kids per court.

Part of the genius of the drilling system in Spain is that the training is almost always like a semi-private lesson, with one player drilling for 20-60 balls, and one player picking up, for example. This way the coach never runs out of balls, and the players get to develop higher levels of shot tolerance, concentration, and stamina, with a good work/rest ratio. I had never seen two kids per court implemented until I traveled to the Spanish academies—and I immediately fell in love with the concept. Even today, in my summer academy, we keep the Spanish ratio—two kids per court. I'm sure we are one of the few academies in the U.S. that does this in summer time. Unfortunately most academies in the summer are focused on making maximum profit by putting as many players as possible on the courts.

In the United States, with so many kids on a court, it's no wonder that the pace and frequency of the way we drill is very different, and the number of repetitions before a break needs to be much lower so players are kept active and don't stand around too much. Inadvertently, by keeping the player-to-court ratio high and the repetitions per drill set low in the United States, we have undermined the training of our players' concentration and shot tolerance. We have essentially adopted a drill style and rhythm that reinforces short attention spans, early aggressiveness rather than patience, and a very low shot tolerance. The long, rhythmic drills in Spain develop the attributes needed to be steady, focused, and patient, all qualities that elite baseline players should have—not just clay court players!

Interestingly, and as a side note, in Spain the coach's feeding carts/baskets hold generally 60-80 balls maximum.

Spanish coaches usually teach out of a small bucket, not a big cart. Rarely are 350 ball carts used in Spain, unlike the United States. With two kids per court, one picking up and one training, the Spanish have figured out a way to use balls more economically than in the United States.

Lluis Bruguera explained to me that by extending his drills for long periods of time, i.e. 20 balls or longer, he works the player's concentration more than if he were to drill for just a few shots at a time. "With my method," he said, "we work more doing a lot of drills. Not two, five, six shots—more and more and more and more..." Long, taxing drills build the concentration and patience of a player, the essential ingredients of shot tolerance development. Pato Alvarez's drills can sometimes reach 100 or more balls without a rest break for the student! It's a brutal and effective method of teaching a player the mental skills to be more consistent.

This kind of training is like an ultra-endurance marathon race, and it really teaches the player to suffer and persevere, important mental qualities that Spanish coaches actively develop, which we will discuss in detail in Chapter 6.

"We create good mentalities," said Albert Costa. "The players are strong mentally and physically. And I think if you grow up on clay or slow hard court, you have to use the legs and, at the end, that's very important."

After drilling hard from the basket on consistency and control, players play and train with live balls on the slow red clay, and the coaches constantly reinforce the values of patience, concentration, and consistency—but never by pushing—always with maximum whip and racquet acceleration.

Classic Spanish Drills To Develop The Three C's: Control, Consistency, and Concentration

Complete video reviews and demonstrations are available online. I encourage readers to visit Secretsofspanishtennis. com and the Chris Lewit YouTube page for more complete explanations of the nuances of the following exercises and to visually see me demonstrating the drills with my students.

Rafael Nadal

3x20 Pato Alvarez

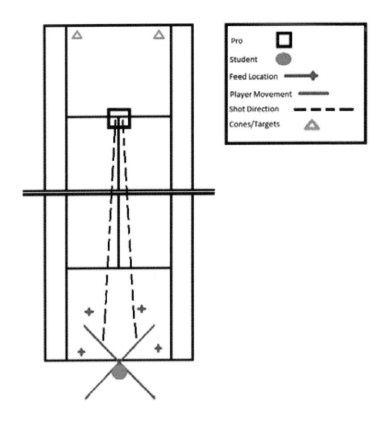

Purpose: To train consistency, accuracy and control, and concentration as well as secondary elements such as stamina, racquet acceleration and footwork and positioning. This is one of the many variations of the wall drill that is used widely in Spain. Pato uses this exercise with players early in the practice to develop groundstrokes rhythm and also at tournaments for a warmup before the match

Key Details:

- The coach should volley softly, floating the ball deep to the baseline, to give the player time to position the feet and accelerate

- The volley can be all deep shots or the coach can volley short and long, developing the in-and-out or X pattern of footwork

- Good balance and positioning to receive the ball "between the hips and shoulders" at the optimal contact point

- Racquet acceleration on every swing

- The player must make every ball to the chest or racquet of the coach, making sure no balls are dropped short at the coach's feet. No Mistakes!

Repetitions: 3 sets of 20 balls in a row. If the player misses, the count restarts at zero

Lluis Bruguera's Wall (Random)

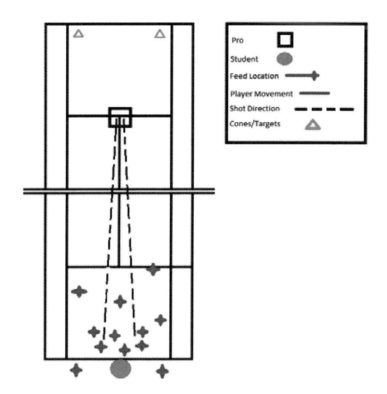

Purpose: Same purpose as above. Bruguera's variation of *la pared* is less structured and can take the player all over the court

Key Details:

- The player needs to read the incoming ball and quickly position the body with balance to "receive the ball"

- Acceleration on every shot

- Depth and accuracy—putting the ball to the coach's racquet

- Concentration – no mistakes!

Repetitions: 20-100 balls in a row. The record at the Bruguera Academy was 840 in a row by Garbine Muguruza

Side-To-Side 20-Ball Drills

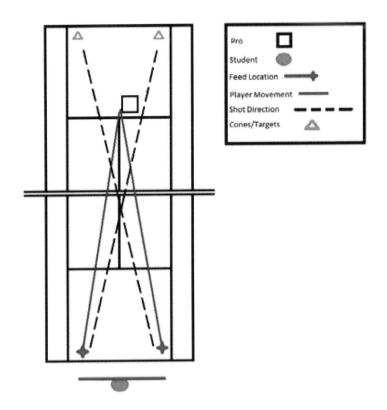

Pro	☐
Student	●
Feed Location	→
Player Movement	—
Shot Direction	- - -
Cones/Targets	△

Purpose: A classic, fundamental Spanish drill that I've seen at various academies. The exercises consist of long and arduous 20 balls or more sets for stamina and consistency, designed to work on the three C's and also perseverance

Key Details:

- Player is working on a deep rally ball and should always position himself on the run to take the ball between hips and shoulders at the optimal contact point out in front of the body and with good distance management

- Player should send the ball with good racquet acceleration, spin, and height to the safe target areas of the court

- Coach can vary the patterns. Common patterns are forehand/backhand, forehand/inverted forehand, inverted backhand and inverted forehand (a Pato Alvarez favorite)

- Coach can vary the pace and spins of the feeds

- Coach feeds with the racquet from across the net or can hand feed from the same side of the net

- The player should make a brief pause to check balance after each shot but still needs to repeatedly recover quickly to get ready for the next shot

- No mistakes!

Repetitions: 20 balls in a row without a mistake is desired. The counting goal can be adjusted by the coach depending on the level of the players, from 10 shots to 30 or more, for very advanced elite juniors or professionals

Jose Higueras Style Cross-Court and Down-the-Lines

Cross-court and down-the-line variations (1 cross-court, 1 down-the-line; 2 cross-court, 1 down-the-line; 3 cross-court, 1 down-the-line; 2 down-the-line, 1 cross-court; and other patterns at the coach's discretion)

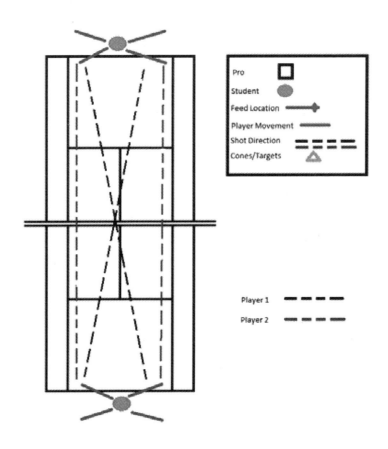

Purpose: Live ball exercises stressing consistent baseline rallying. These exercises are very popular in Spain and generally use the classic Spanish counting method of structuring the drill. For example, the players must reach 20 balls in a row and any mistake restarts the exercise, or another variation of counting for a consistency focus

Key Details:

- The focus of these exercises will support and reinforce the coach's work with the players during the drills. The players should work on good balance and positioning to receive the ball well, manage a perfect contact point, and then send the ball with maximum racquet acceleration. Higueras favors working on these patterns regularly to develop better ball control and consistency

- Depth and safe rallying is key. The players should strive to keep the ball deep into the corners of the court and to play with margin away from the lines

- Players should work at a very high intensity level, running for every ball until exhaustion—this is very important to train the discipline, suffering, and stamina aspect

- The coach can also call "play the point" at any time for variation and engagement! The players would compete for one point and then restart the exercise

Repetitions: From 10-40 balls The counting goal can be adjusted by the coach depending on the level of the players. The exercises can also be based on time

Toni Nadal Style Cross-Court and Down-the-Lines

Cross-court and down-the-line variations (1 cross-court, 1 down-the-line; 2 cross-court, 1 down-the-line; 3 cross-court, 1 down-the-line; 2 down-the-line, 1 cross-court and other patterns at the coach's discretion)

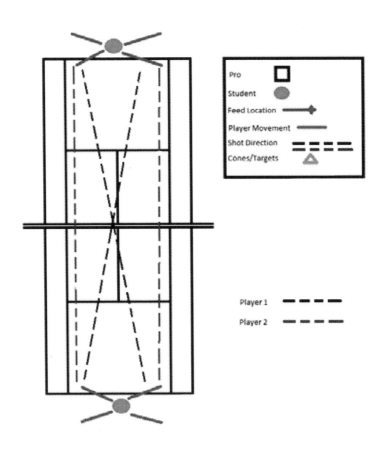

Purpose: Toni Nadal puts his spin on traditional live ball pattern exercises by limiting the sequence of shots and then playing the point after a certain number of hits in the pattern. By incorporating an element of competition and game play within the exercise, the player engagement tends to be better and the drills are less boring and dry

Key Details:

- The focus of these types of live ball exercises will support and reinforce the coach's work with the players during the hand and racquet fed drills. The players should work on good balance and positioning to receive the ball well, manage a perfect contact point, and then send the ball with maximum racquet acceleration

- Depth and safe rallying is key. The players should strive to keep the ball deep into the corners of the court and to play with margin away from the lines

- Toni likes to prescribe short 3-6 ball rallies with many different patterns. For example, one player will play down-the-line and the other cross-court. If 4 shots are made with control, the players would play the point with no restrictions

- Toni likes to play short games to 5 or 7 points total

Repetitions: Shorter repetitions (3-6 stroke rallies) within a pattern combined with point play

Uncle Toni's Favorite Control Game

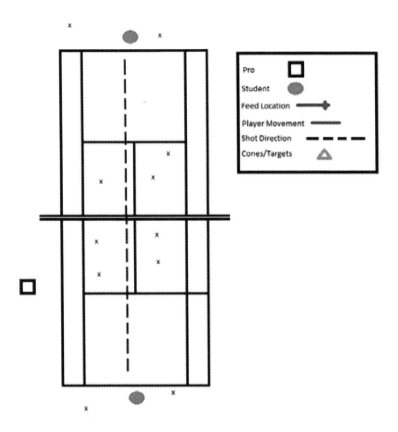

Purpose: To develop control, consistency, and depth

Key Details:

- This is a classic Toni Nadal tactical game. He has many good ones that he incorporates into the practices at the Rafa Nadal Academy

- This is a live ball game with a player feeding one point each in alternating fashion for fairness

- The ball must be hit down an imaginary middle lane of the court. No dropshots or angles allowed

- If a player misses long past the baseline, she would lose two points. If a player misses in the service box, it's a warning and the play keeps going. If a player misses twice in the service box, one point goes to the opponent

Repetitions: Toni likes to score the game to 5 or 7 points to create focus and pressure. Multiple short games can be played: 2 out of 3 sets or 3 out of 5 grand slam format

One Player In Corner, One Grinds

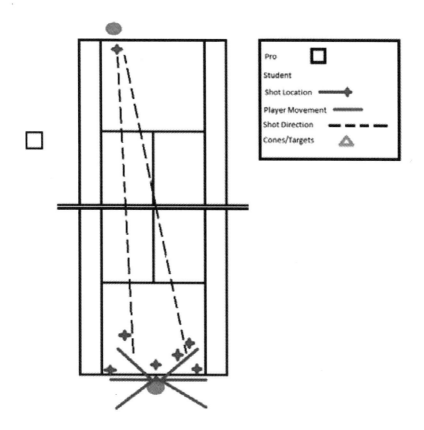

Purpose: A favorite at many Spanish academies, this exercise works on the consistency of the rally ball and also some defensive shots

Key Details:

- One player must fight and persevere for 20 shots in a row, only targeting one area of the court. If the running player misses, the count must start again. The coach can also use other numerical methods for the drill, such as 20 balls total for less advanced players

- The stationary player will work on positioning for a perfect contact point and changing the direction of the ball without hitting a winner. He should not be lazy with his feet

- The stationary player can be placed on the advantage side of the court to work inside-out and inside-in forehand, a common setup in Spain

- Players should strive to keep every ball in the court, chase down every ball, and always try to get one more ball over the net

- When one player successfully grinds 20, the players switch roles

Repetitions: Try to work towards 20 balls in a row without a mistake. 8 or 10 to start is a good entry level goal

Jofre Porta No Winners Game

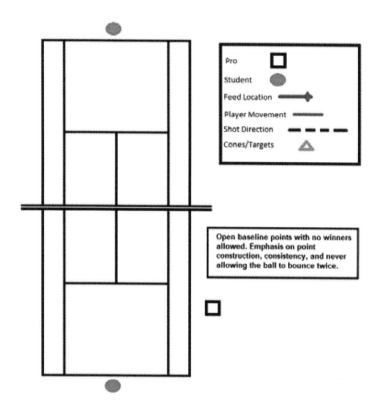

Purpose: To develop patience and control in a game format

Key Details:

- No winners game is a famous game played all around Spain on the slow red dirt

- Baseline game where players grind out points. Winners are not allowed. Dropshots are not allowed. Not chasing balls is not allowed

- The only way to win a point is by the opponent's error. If a player hits a winner, the point is replayed

- If a player does not chase a ball or give maximum effort, he loses the point at the coach's discretion

- At Jofre's academy, if a player does not give maximum effort, he will probably find himself running laps in the parking lot!

Repetitions: Games can be scored from 7 to 10 points, for example

High String Baseline Game

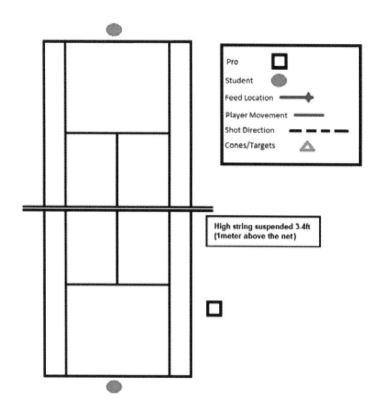

Purpose: A commonly played consistency game all across Spain that teaches players to play with shape and margin over the net

Key Details:

- Each player must hit above a high line or rope strung across the net and connected to two sticks

- Baseline game where players grind out points

- If a player hits below the high string or rope, the point is lost

- If a player does not chase a ball, he loses the point at the coach's discretion

Repetitions: Games can be scored from 7 to 21 points, for example

The Spanish Way—Develop A High Shot Tolerance

Patience and consistency are the hallmarks of a good Spanish player. In Spain, they have developed a system to make the players more patient and consistent, based on many of the exercises and the philosophy described in this chapter. The philosophy and drills discussed are easily adaptable to any training program. Working on the basic rally consistency of a player will undoubtedly improve his or her confidence and reduce anxieties on the court. A player with solid, consistent groundstrokes and a high shot tolerance will have a chance to persevere and win, even when his serve is off or he is having a bad day—and this is a key part of the Spanish method: winning even when playing poorly. Players with a big serve and attack game will be able to succeed on a high level, but they will always be limited in their game patterns and somewhat erratic in their results, because they rely so much on serve and groundstroke winners. It is smart to develop a big serve and attack game, but players can be even more successful if they buttress such a game with consistency—and of course, good defense—which is the next Spanish secret.

CHAPTER 4

Defense

"Defense is fundamental to tennis, because most shots in tennis are playable"
—*Pato Alvarez*

There is a saying in sports such as American football and basketball that "defense wins championships." If this is true in tennis as well, then the Spanish have found a way to win a lot of championships by training defense better than any other country or system in the world.

Spanish players are the masters of defensive tennis. From an early age, players are taught patience, consistency, and concentration, as discussed in Chapter 3. In addition to those principles, defending the ball is another subject that is uniformly taught at all levels. The red clay courts, the second teacher, are again a big factor in the development of a great defensive game. The clay allows players to neutralize big shots, grind, defend, and recover from disadvantageous positions like no other playing surface. Therefore by growing up on clay, Spanish players develop unparalleled defensive capacities. Is it any wonder that Patrick McEnroe, the former head of USTA Player Development for many years, made it a priority to train more top American juniors on clay courts?

In contrast to some other developmental systems that emphasize taking the ball on the rise or "holding the ground" near the baseline and refusing to back up, in Spain players are allowed and encouraged to defend into the far recesses of the court deep behind the baseline. This contrast of styles reminds me of a similar contrast in martial arts systems. In the martial arts, of which I am an avid student, there are some styles known as "hard" or "striking" styles of fighting, and some styles known as "soft" or "gentle" styles of fighting. Karate from Japan or Tae Kwon Do from Korea are hard styles emphasizing the application of direct force against force, energy against energy. By contrast, Judo and Aikido, also from Japan, and Brazilian Jiu Jitsu, for example, are grappling styles which are generally philosophically opposed to the direct application of force to force. These arts are known as gentle arts not because they are not lethal (they are very lethal!), but because they tend to use technique, leverage, and advantageous positioning in a fight to win, rather than direct force. These martial arts try to use energy as efficiently as possible and to use the opponent's force against them whenever possible. Spanish tennis methodology stresses the same efficient use of energy through patient positioning to dominate one's opponent, just like in Brazilian Jiu Jitsu. The Spanish coaches will teach their players to retreat and give up territory in response to a threat, and Spanish players become very good at retreating and defending tough shots as a result of this habitual training.

In Spain, players are taught not to force the court position regardless of the type of ball hit. Rather, players must move fluidly and adjust court position always in response to their reading of the depth, pace, and spin of the incoming shot. Carlos Alcaraz demonstrates this "give and take" better than any other modern Spanish player It is the constant reading and then adjustment and movement from defense to neutral to offense, or vice versa that typifies the Spanish style of training—and gives them an edge in baseline battles.

Different Court Positions

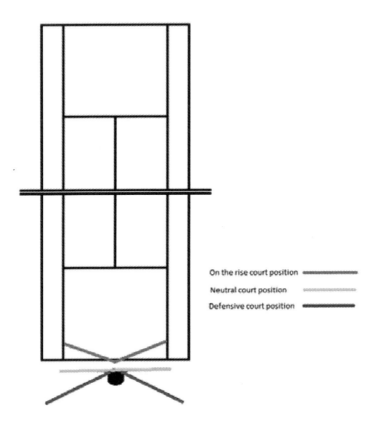

On the rise court position ━━━━━━
Neutral court position ┅┅┅┅┅┅
Defensive court position ━━━━━━

Spanish players traditionally do not want to be caught "fighting the ball," a common coaching phrase. Fighting the ball means standing your ground and taking the ball early rather than moving back into a better position to receive the ball. It's the direct application of force versus force. As mentioned before, the Spanish want to use energy efficiently, and they don't want to waste energy fighting a difficult ball from the baseline when they can back up, let the force die out, and then send the ball more effectively (heavier and with more height and spin) from a deep position. Says Jose Higueras, "If someone tries to punch me in the face, I'm going to back up and not just stand there and get hit. The Spanish coaches are generally obsessed with "receiving the ball" properly, and this is the reason that footwork and movement training is so paramount to their system (see Chapter 1).

If you go to an academy like Bardou Competition or Emilio Sánchez Academy, the system is traditional in the sense that the players are taught to go back and defend routinely; taking the ball early is generally discouraged. Half-volley type groundstrokes are a big faux pas for Spanish players taught in the traditional way. However, at more progressive academies like Rafa Nadal Academy, JC Ferrero or BTT (Barcelona Total Tennis), the players tend to take the ball relatively early while still maintaining the classic defensive style when necessary— there is a balanced or nuanced approach. Indeed, I observed that many of the players were taking the ball from a court position generally much closer to the baseline at Ferrero Tennis Academy, for example, than the players at Emilio Sánchez or Bardou. Players from BTT, for example, are specifically taught to take the ball earlier than some other academies in Spain, according to director Jordi Vilaró, former Davis Cup coach of Spain. Carlos Alcaraz is a paragon of the JC Ferrero style. On a recent visit, he could be observed working on taking the ball very early and his court position was right on top of the baseline in preparation for the grass court season.

This is a good example of the traditional Spanish approach evolving and being tweaked and updated by the next generation of Spanish coaches. Many Spanish coaches are aware of their past and are wary of being categorized as "clay court specialists." The modern coaching establishment wants to develop great players on all surfaces, not just great clay court players.

Therefore there is a contrast between the traditional Spanish way of defending (until your opponents wear out), and the more modern or progressive Spanish way which still values defense and grinding, but adjusts court position somewhat closer to the baseline and preaches more aggressiveness using the all-court game more frequently. Toni Nadal's method is much more aggressive than Lluis Bruguera's style, for example.

As Bruguera has said, "With this system every player has a good forehand, good backhand, good footwork, good control, and he can play. It's possible he won't lose." However, this traditional Spanish philosophy, while an excellent start and foundation, may not be enough *to win* in today's power game. More and more, players need to have an offensive mindset and capability to complete their games.

Another example of this growing evolution was when Andy Murray broke with his travel coach Pato Alvarez, the legendary Spanish coach, reportedly because Andy felt that the advice and strategies Pato was giving him were too defensive and reactionary; he wanted a coach to support a more proactive, aggressive all-court style. More recently, Carlos Alcaraz demonstrates the prototypical modern Spanish player: aggressive with a solid all-court game and an ability to vary his court position as required, including taking the ball very early.

Keys To Defending Well In The Spanish Style

In Spain, defense does not just mean getting the ball back over the net. In many instances, the coaches will emphasize an "aggressive defense," which means using a lot of racquet speed to send the ball deep into the corners to neutralize the opponent's shot. An aggressive defense is typified by heavy spin, depth, and penetration, and this type of shot will allow the Spanish player not just to stay in the point, but many times the player will be able to escape from a disadvantageous position and obtain an advantageous court position from which to attack as the point progresses.

Learning to accelerate and "hit out" from defensive positions is a concept routinely stressed by Spanish coaches, and Spanish players are always looking for opportunities to regain court position to go on the attack, even when they are in a defensive position and in trouble. It can be very difficult to master the skill of aggressive defense for players who grow up on hard courts and are not used to defending with good racquet speed.

The capacity to go from neutral to defense, to neutral, and then to offense is a key characteristic of top Spanish juniors and pros. On the clay, the game of tennis becomes a chess match, with each player moving the other into advantageous or disadvantageous positions and ultimately looking for the opportunity to win the point or force an error by attrition. This style of play is in stark contrast with American style tennis, or tennis from any country dominated by fast courts, such as England, where the game is less of a chess match and more of a shooting match—a game of attack and winners. In those one dimensional systems, players are not trained, nor are they afforded many opportunities (due to the fast surfaces played on) to transition back and forth from defense to offense and vice versa all within the scope of a single point. That kind of positional and tactical flexibility and versatility is a hallmark of Spain's multidimensional development system, and Spanish players are taught these skills both by the clay and systematically through the use of many defensive and transitional drills. Indeed, as discussed earlier in the book, frequently players from fast court regions move to Spain to learn how to play tennis better tactically—to become better tennis "chess" players.

Drills To Cultivate The Defensive Game

Pato's Defensive V

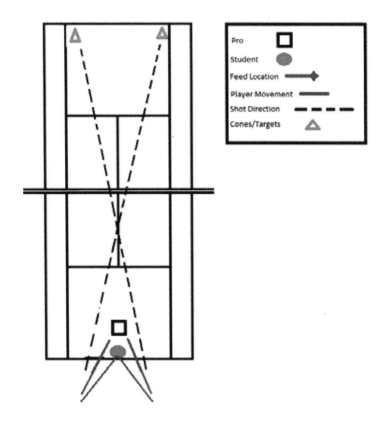

Purpose: To push a player deep into the back of the court, forcing him to hit a difficult high bouncing shot, challenging the player's footwork and positioning. The exercise trains the player to hit with length from an extreme defensive position

Key Details:

- Tactical key is to hit with depth into the safe deep zones of the court, either crosscourt or down the line

- Technically the player must work the feet and shuffle into position (Pato prefers the double-rhythm style of movement) to get a good contact point between hip and shoulder

- Racquet speed is important to get a heavy spin on the defensive shot

- Player should load weight on the back leg and can jump backward if necessary

- Recover back to the baseline after successfully defending

- Pato often racquet feeds from the same side of the net as the player, or hand feeding can be used. Racquet feeding upward or downward can apply more pace on the ball and pressure on the player

Repetitions: 10-20+ balls

Bruguera Deep Defense Drill

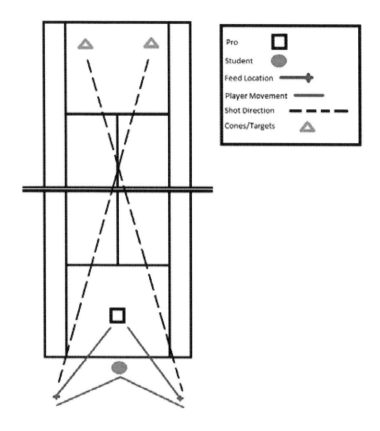

Purpose: To train the emergency defensive lateral movement on deeper balls, moving deep diagonally to receive the ball. This drill is a bit slower in tempo and rhythm than the Emergency Drill discussed in the first chapter

Key Details:

- Players are encouraged to run back to a deep position and load the legs well. In Spain, they commonly preach "load the back leg!"

- Coach can isolate either forehand or backhand side, or combine both sides

- Good recovery after making the shot back to the house, or *casa*

- Tactically, a high and deep defensive topspin shot to the safe zones of the court is key

- Generally hand fed in the Bruguera style

Repetitions: 10-10 repetitions fed at a slow, regular cadence

The Classic Spanish Full X Drill

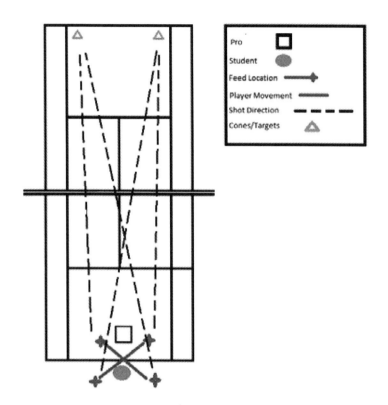

Purpose: An integrated drill that can work many areas of the development of the player: technical, tactical, physical and mental. For the focus of this chapter, the defense can certainly be stressed more than offense to develop better defensive shots. One of the most famous drills in Spain used by Lluis Bruguera and Pato Alvarez and adapted around the country by other leading coaches

Key Details:

- The coach can focus on the transition from offense to defense and should emphasize the proper neutralizing of the incoming ball using high and deep topspin

- Good footwork and positioning are key to setting up to send the ball deep on the defense

- Tactically, the coach can train different patterns, such as crosscourt attack and down-the-line defense, which was the way Pato Alvarez liked to train his players, or the player can make their own decisions on the shot based on the incoming ball (more Bruguera style)

- Racquet speed on the defensive shot and on the offensive attack

- Good balance and body control

Repetitions: 20-100

Toni Nadal Random Defense

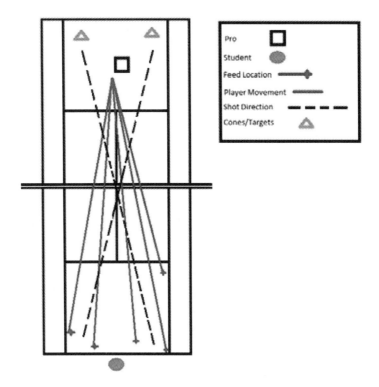

Purpose: This is a creative exercise from the mind of Uncle Toni that consists of regular rally shots combined with a very difficult, surprise scrambling defensive shot. The purpose is to train the eyes and awaken the player's nervous system so that he or she is ready to move quickly for any defensive tactical situation that may arise

Key Details:

- The coach feeds easier balls to rally and then randomly fires a fast difficult ball anywhere on the court. The player must chase! Following the random shot, the coach resumes easy feeding again

- Toni stresses awareness and hustle. The player must be ready for the defensive surprise ball and chase with maximum effort. No laziness

- The player must work the legs and feet well on the rally shots to achieve the optimal position to receive the ball

- A second variation is the player attacks several balls in a defined pattern with one random defensive scrambling shot interspersed in the sequence

Repetitions: 12-30 or more balls

Toni Nadal Attack and Defense

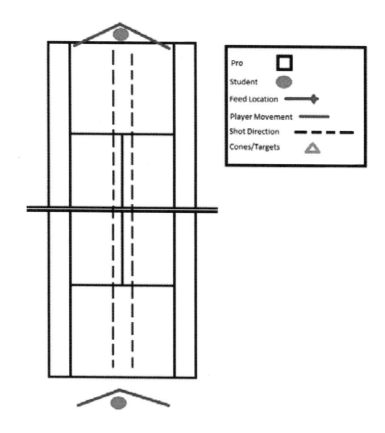

Purpose: A wonderful live ball exercise to develop the "give and take"—one player tries to improve his position and attack while the other defends and retrieves

Key Details:

- The players hit rally balls with control down the middle through an imaginary center lane in the court. No angles or winners to the side are allowed

- The attacking player tries to hold and improve his court position, hitting strong from closer and closer to the baseline or inside the baseline when possible

- The defending player retrieves and gives ground and works on sending an aggressive defense—high and heavy spin neutralizing shots when possible

- Racquet speed is important on the defensive shots and on the offensive shots

- Good balance and body control on defense

- Scoring can be incorporated to create a competitive game. Toni likes to play short games with the winner reaching 5 or 7 points

Repetitions: Games to 5 or 7 points. The exercise can be timed rather than scored, with players alternating roles for time. For example, one player works two minutes on offense and then switch

Never Neglect Defensive Training

An important takeaway from the Spanish method is to incorporate defensive training methods into every training curriculum. Even if players like to attack, it will benefit them to boost their defensive capabilities, so that when pressed, they can neutralize and have a chance to earn points under duress. Players who work on their defense develop a more well-rounded game, can play and win even when being attacked by a bigger, stronger player, and have more versatile games that can allow them to win more points against a variety of opponent game styles and in difficult match conditions.

Over the past decades, Spanish coaches have become masters at training the defensive game. The Spanish model of training is currently the best in the world at teaching how to defend, counterpunch and neutralize. Players may not need to train defense as regularly—or even with such a high priority as in Spain—but all players, even very aggressive ones, would benefit by having a portion of their training focused on the subjects in the Spanish defensive curriculum. Unfortunately, many countries, including the United States, have neglected to promote and develop these types of important defensive skills to the detriment of their players.

CHAPTER 5

Physical Conditioning

"Very few Spanish players are really tall and so not many of them can serve at over 200 kilometers an hour all the time so they have to work really hard from the back of the court and so they need to be in great condition. Before, players would spend 90 percent of the time hitting balls and then maybe go for a run or train on the bike, whereas now their training is based on almost 50 percent tennis and 50 percent conditioning. That's how important it has become."
—Javier Piles, Professional Spanish Coach

Spanish players and coaches have figured out that the modern tennis game is a physical game generally where the strongest, fastest, fittest, and most powerful athlete usually wins. The Spanish understand that if they build superior athletes who are more agile, quicker, can run longer without getting tired, and stay injury free, they can develop those athletes into world-class tennis players. In many other countries, including the United States, building tennis players seems to be the main focus—not building athletes. By building athletes first and tennis players second, Spain has figured out the formula for maximizing the performance of the talent pool they have in their tennis system.

In the 1980s legendary Spanish coaches like Lluis Bruguera and Pato Alvarez anticipated the trend towards serious physical training for tennis at a time when most tennis players just played sets and practiced with very little serious off-court conditioning. Players like Ivan Lendl and Jim Courier (who had a Spanish coach for many years, Jose Higueras), who were on the vanguard of the trend toward serious physical conditioning, taught the world about how important getting fit was to high performance on the tennis court. In that time period, however, the Spanish were already well on their way towards recognizing this trend, and they systematized this philosophy nationwide much earlier than other countries did. The dividends from this prescience were huge and made Spain a dominant force in the tennis world.

When Sergi Bruguera burst on the scene in the early 1990s, he was known as being one of the fittest guys on the tour; he could run all day long like a deer without getting tired. Arantxa Sánchez Vicario, who won the French Open in 1989 and reached No. 1 in the world in 1995, also stood out for her incredible fitness level and ability to run. This became the new Spanish paragon. Pato and Lluis made serious off-court physical training an important component of their new training systems and the repercussions can still be seen today in the methodologies at modern Spanish academies. Spanish academies are the only training centers I know that essentially split each training day almost 50/50 into off-court fitness sessions and on-court tennis. It is not uncommon for players to log up to three hours of fitness and 2-3 hours of tennis during a heavy conditioning-periodized schedule or even more fitness during preseason training, which is usually 6-8 weeks in November or December. In Spain, the academies take preseason training very seriously. Outside of preseason, Spanish academies typically only train 3-3.5 hours on the tennis court and 2-2.5 hours in the gym, running, working agility, stretching and performing injury prevention, etc.

Sergi Bruguera

In contrast, the typical American program is 4-5 hours of tennis and maybe one hour of conditioning, but the conditioning oftentimes seems to be just tacked on like an afterthought at most training centers—it's not the PRIORITY! The Spanish really prioritize off-court training. It is at the heart of their system and philosophy because if a player is not injury free and strong at the end of a match, he cannot win, especially a match on red clay.

On a recent visit to Ferrero Tennis Academy, the author was lucky enough to observe Carlos Alcaraz training in the gym for several days. While the gym at the academy was basic and did not have much in terms of fancy equipment and the latest techno gadgetry, the workouts were professionally managed and orchestrated by the elite trainers there. Alcaraz trained hard like a beast for performance and also spent important time with his trainers focusing on injury prevention. It's very typical all across Spain to see a relatively simple gym and fitness setup but extremely intense and professional training. Global Tennis Academy has a very simple gym, too, but the trainers there are excellent. Two exceptions are the Emilio Sánchez Academy and Rafa Nadal Academy where the gym centers are very modern and cutting-edge—and the training is super professional, of course, as well.

Preseason

All professionally-run Spanish academies that I have visited have a serious preseason training program, usually in November to December that lasts 6-8 weeks in preparation for the new year of the ITF circuit and the Australian Open in

January. During preseason, the first week or two, sometimes the players don't even play tennis, they just spend 3-4 hours running, in the gym, or doing injury prevention work. The rest of preseason, the schedule each week titrates one to two hours of tennis each day while still training intensely off the court. In this manner, at least once per year, players dedicate themselves nearly one hundred percent to preventing injuries, getting stronger and quicker, and building stamina.

This type of macro-periodization is very important and can help prevent injuries and improve performance over the long-term, especially for players who follow this kind of schedule year after year from a young age. In the United States, most coaches, academies, and top level juniors do not have the same commitment to fitness and injury prevention. The United States pays a dear price—both with injuries and also on the performance side of the equation. Very few American nationally-ranked juniors actually have a periodized schedule with 6-8 weeks dedicated solely to injury prevention and getting fitter. We would be much better off in this country if we did.

As an American high performance coach myself, having trained multiple No.1 nationally ranked players and many top ten nationally ranked players, I can say from first-hand experience that it is difficult—near impossible—to convince American parents to ease back on the tennis to work on the physical condition of their player. This phenomenon may be one of the reasons we see an epidemic of repetitive stress injuries at the junior tournament level in the United States. There is too much tournament tennis and not enough time devoted to injury prevention and getting stronger. One major issue is that we hold two prestigious junior events—Eddie Herr and Orange

Bowl in December—a time of year when Spanish players typically rest and grow stronger. There needs to be more tournament breaks in the United States and a well-defined preseason period when all American juniors stop hitting balls and hit the gym to get stronger and, most importantly, prevent injuries.

Sample Preseason Training Day

Spain is exceptional in the quality of its preseason training. Coaches and players take preseason very seriously. Preseason overloads fitness and individual physical conditioning and reduces the amount of tennis time. Typically matches are not played. The intensity on the court is lowered while off-court training intensity and volume is increased. Preseason usually lasts 6-8 weeks in Spain. Adding periodized, targeted preseason blocks of training into an annual schedule allows time to work towards important athletic and physical development goals.

Preseason Schedule

7:45am
- Dynamic warm up

8-10
- Physical conditioning: Lifting for strength and power is typical. Priority given to improving specific areas such as stamina, speed and agility or power based on individual assessments

10-1130

- Tennis training: Drills and skill development. Movement and groundstrokes focus. Basket drills focus. Deprioritization of live ball hitting and points

- Footwork cleaning

1130-12
- Static stretching

12-1
- Lunch

1-230pm
- Fitness with a mobility, stability and flexibility focus

230-4
- Tennis training. Specific basket work. Limited live ball exercises. Focus on improving strengths and buttressing weaknesses

4-430
- Recovery swim in the pool for metabolic flushing

5-6pm
- Recreational soccer game

Injury Prevention

Getting faster, stronger, and building stamina is great, but the Spanish have a great appreciation for injury prevention work and take their prehabilitation training very seriously. It was Pat Etcheberry, renowned fitness trainer who said, "The most important goal of a serious off-court conditioning program is to prevent injuries, not improve performance. Injury prevention is the priority." I think the best Spanish coaches and trainers believe in the same approach, and they started a serious injury prevention regimen years before other countries did.

In Spain, players generally spend fewer hours on court per week—usually between 15-20 hours tennis—less than at some other academies, but they spend probably 5-10 more hours working injury prevention and conditioning. Indeed, many observers are shocked to learn that the Spanish players don't typically train more than 3-3.5 hours per day of tennis. This unique approach to training develops players who are rarely overtrained on the court, have fewer repetitive stress injuries, are more resistant to burnout, and are strong and fit when it comes down to that critical third or fifth set.

Injury Prevention Exercises Common In Spain

Core and Lower Back
It's important to train the abdominals and paraspinals to develop a strong "muscle corset."

Rotator Cuff

The supraspinatus, infraspinatus, teres minor, and subscapularis are the four rotator cuff muscles that every tennis player should understand anatomically. These important muscles secure the glenohumeral joint and help the shoulder move in many directions to swing the racquet. No injury prevention protocol is complete without rotator cuff strength building.

Scapular Mobility

Research shows that athletes who use repeated overhead shoulder movements can suffer from reduced internal shoulder rotation range of motion (ROM) and increased external shoulder rotation ROM. Studies suggest that if the ratio of internal shoulder rotation ROM to external rotation ROM exceeds certain parameters that athletes are at increased risk of shoulder injuries. Scapular mobility exercises are critical to maintaining a healthy shoulder rotation ratio.

Yoga

Yoga is a very popular way to work on long-term flexibility in Spain. Yoga or general stretching can fill a fitness session with a functional, non-impact workout.

Hip Mobility

Hip mobility training is very common in Spain and helps players move with more agility and quickness. Alcaraz is an example of a Spanish player with great hip mobility, which he works on every week at his academy, Ferrero Tennis Academy.

Ankle Stability

Oftentimes ankle stability is forgotten in the gym—but not in Spain. Ankle stability is important for Spanish players in particular because of all the sliding they do on clay courts.

Recovery Modalities

Common In Spain

Indiba Treatment

Indiba uses an electromagnetic current to increase muscle tissue temperature and improve blood flow to increase healing. It's a popular treatment in Spain and prominently used at the Ferrero Tennis Academy and Rafa Nadal Academy.

Ultrasound Treatment

Ultrasound therapy is generally used to treat inflammations and repair tissues. Many elite academies in Spain offer ultrasound therapy.

Compression Therapy

Compression technology (like Normatec Legs) by companies like Hyperice have become popular in Spain and can increase circulation, reduce swelling and soreness in muscles.

Sports Cryotherapy

Elite training centers like Rafa Nadal Academy offer Cryosense cold chambers to maximize recovery.

Anti-Gravity Treadmills

Advanced machines like AlterG treadmills, used at the Rafa Nadal Academy, feature NASA Differential Air Pressure (DAP) technology and real-time gait analysis. These treadmills can reduce the amount of impact loading on the joints and can be valuable when recovering from injury.

Contrast Bathing

Contrast bathing, used at the Rafael Nadal Academy for example, is the alternating use of hot and cold immersion to reduce inflammation and promote metabolic waste removal.

Swimming

Using the ocean and pools, this inexpensive and low-tech form of hydrotherapy is common in Spain as a way to speed recovery.

Racquet Speed and Power Development

Just as Spanish coaches on the court are obsessed with racquet speed and power, the same dedication to building these qualities can be found in the Spanish trainers who work in the gym and off the court with the players. Spain has many excellent physical trainers and physiotherapists with experience at high levels of professional sport. Having a knowledgeable, educated, and certified sport science staff ready and available is a real asset for the Spanish players. At the former Bruguera Academy, for example, experienced professional trainers like Salvador Sosa, who traveled many years on the professional tour and worked with players like Alex Corretja, Ivan Ljubicic and Andrea Gaudenzi, supervised excellent training programs for their charges. These kinds of sport science and athletic training experts are critical to the Spanish method and can be found at all of the top academies. The elite athletic trainers are perhaps the hidden force behind Spanish tennis success.

Spanish athletic coaches focus on developing power and racquet speed with cables, bands, medicine balls, and other innovative devices like the VersaPulley and other technologies. Spain's athletic training community is on the cutting-edge and is often leading the rest of the world with innovative training ideas and progressive approaches to physical training and injury prevention. Rafa Nadal Academy and Ferrero Tennis Academy, for example, are two of the top academies in Spain when it comes to incorporating the latest technologies for training and medicine in their programs.

Many of the expert Spanish trainers work in other professional sports too, like soccer, which is the most popular sport in Spain. In general, the whole sporting culture in Spain has created a high demand for elite sports trainers and the country has plenty available for its athletes. Interestingly, leading Spanish sport scientist Jaime Fernandez-Fernandez, PhD, who worked as an educational consultant for the Royal Spanish Tennis Federation (RFET), says in a personal interview that even today Spanish trainers and coaches could improve their evidence-based practice in the country. It seems there may be a dichotomy in the strength and conditioning field in Spain: The elite trainers are there, but there is a lack of scientific approach for many of the trainers around the country outside of the top academies that I have visited over the years. At the end of this chapter we will detail some basic exercises to help develop the racquet speed off the court and feature them in videos online too.

Acceleration Training In Spain

Wind Exercises

Trainers and coaches will of ten have players swing the racquet at top speed without actually hitting a ball. Sets of wind exercises are a great way to develop explosive racquet speed. Lighter racquets and implements can also be used to develop the sensation of whipping.

Medicine Ball Rotations

The medicine ball is commonly used to develop a strong foundation in the lower body and to develop the leg drive and hip rotation needed to accelerate the racquet quickly.

Cable Machine Rotations

Cable machines in the gym are used in Spain to mimic the movements of the groundstroke and serve. Light weights can be used when explosive power is the goal or heavier weights can be used at slower speeds to develop strength.

VersaPulley

VersaPulley is a variable-resistance flywheel machine that can enhance sports movement and athletic training through eccentric and inertial resistance. The device is common in Spanish gyms. Players can simulate strokes with variable resistance using the VersaPulley machine.

Isokinetic Machines

Advanced isokinetic resistance machines can be used to train acceleration at constant speeds with variable resistance. These machines can also be used for rehabilitation.

Resistance Bands

Resistance bands are commonly used in Spain for acceleration work that simulates the tennis swings. Bands are also used for mobility and rotator cuff strengthening.

Stroops Accelerations

The Stroops bungee, popular in Spain, is often combined with racquet acceleration work to develop the stability of the athlete during high speed swings.

Stamina

Of course stamina work has been a standard part of
Spanish training for decades. Spanish players are famous world-
wide for their endurance and never-quit attitude. While it seems
the rest of the world athletic training community has dismissed
distance running as inefficient and problematic for tennis
players, most academies that I visited used running as a standard
part of their training system, although some academies, like
Ferrero Tennis Academy and Rafa Nadal Academy, are starting
to focus less on distance work and more on short intervals and
multi-directional speed. Jaime Fernandez-Fernandez says that
this is an important trend in Spanish fitness practice. Contrast
the emphasis on running in Spain to the US where many of
our tennis players do not run ever. I have many students who
have come to my training center who have admitted to me that
they have never even run a mile in their lives! It seems that the
simple Spanish running focus, whether for distance or shorter
intervals, has made the players there very strong in terms of
endurance and cardiovascular capacity.

At the former Bruguera Academy, for example, running
was a regular part of the training regimen and, once or twice
a week, the players would even run the mountain nearby to
develop stamina and perseverance (the all-important willingness
to suffer, which will be discussed in the next chapter). At Emilio
Sánchez Academy in Barcelona, the players used to run weekly
and also at the former TennisVal (now Lozano-Altur Academy)
in Valencia, I was greeted—surprise, surprise—by a group of
players out for a stamina run. At Global Tennis in Mallorca,
Jofre Porta still believes in running, and many of the kids there

are punished for misbehavior or lack of effort, with running challenges. The Spanish understand that, fundamentally, running helps build the cardio base needed to win on clay, but more importantly, I believe Spanish trainers often use good old-fashioned running, especially distance running to develop the willingness to suffer—the mental toughness—which is a critical part of the Spanish method of training.

Tennis specific footwork, as discussed in Chapter 1, tends to be trained on the court by the coaches, but off the court coaches will work on agility and coordination with ladders, cones, etc. These kinds of training are not unique to Spain; they can be seen at every academy around the world. The on-court footwork and movement drills (also detailed in Chapter One) are the real secrets of the Spanish way. What makes Spanish physical conditioning different is the prioritization of the training, the extra volume of training (more time per week dedicated), the focus on injury prevention, stamina, and particularly racquet speed development.

Endurance Training Common In Spain

On-Court Drills

The grueling on-court exercises that Spanish coaches have made famous are the most common way to build endurance in Spain.

Distance Running

While many modern trainers in Spain are moving away from traditional distance training for stamina, the good old-fashioned 3k to 5k run—and sometimes longer distances—is still commonly used for cross-training.

Intervals

Interval training that mimics the work-rest ratio on the tennis court is also a common method of building cardiovascular fitness for tennis.

Soccer Cross-Training

Soccer is part of the cultural fabric of Spain and played fervently and frequently, which helps build cardiovascular endurance of participants.

Agility and Coordination Exercises Common In Spain

As mentioned in Chapter 1, movement skills are often integrated into the tennis training sessions in Spain. Trainers complement the on-court tennis footwork training with off-court and on court agility and coordination work.

Agility Ladder

In Spain, agility ladder work is popular particularly with the added stimuli of throwing and catching a ball, bouncing a ball, or other concurrent coordination task.

Soccer Skills

Soccer is the most popular sport in Spain and many tennis players cross-train on the soccer field. The extra soccer ball kicking and trapping, and the foot coordination that is developed in soccer, can improve tennis court movement and agility.

Sliding

Many fitness sessions in Spain are performed on the clay court. Sliding practice on the clays trengthens the adductors, quadriceps, and hamstrings, and enhances coordination and balance.

Stroops

The Stroops bungee is a fantastic and popular device used in movement training drills all across Spain, both on the court and off the court.

Examples of various Spanish injury prevention, acceleration, stamina, and sliding exercises are featured at the book website

What's A Typical Training Week Like In Spain?

Here is a typical training week in Spain. Remember that cleaning footwork, balance, and movement typically takes place daily. In Spain, the fitness component can reach 50 percent of the daily training load. Soccer is often played after the practice day for fun and that adds some additional fitness and footwork benefits. Some academies train six days a week with half days Wednesday and Saturday (Sunday off) while others train Monday through Friday full days with the weekend off. The schedule below will give you a sense of how the day flows and a taste of what the typical training week is like for serious Spanish players:

Monday
7:45am
- Dynamic warm up

8-10
- Tennis training: Drills and skill development. Movement and groundstrokes focus. Cleaning the technique and footwork after weekend competitions.

Basket focus and some live ball exercises

10-1130

- Physical conditioning: Circuit strength training routine

1130-12

- Static stretching

12-1

- Lunch

1-230pm

- Tennis: Typically live ball points and set play with a strategic focus

230-4

- Fitness with a mobility, stability and flexibility focus
- Core and lower back work
- Scapular mobility
- Hip mobility
- Static stretching

4-430

- Recovery in the pool. Light swimming for metabolic flushing

5-6

- Recreational soccer game

Tuesday

7:45am

- Dynamic warm up

8-10

- Tennis training: Drills and skill development. Movement and groundstrokes focus. Consistency. Basket focus and some live ball exercises

10-1130

- Physical conditioning: Speed and agility training. Coordination training

1130-12

- Static stretching

12-1 lunch

1-230pm

- Tennis: Typically live ball points and set play with a tactical focus

230-4

- Stamina training with a distance run. Yoga or stretching and mobility

4-430

- Recovery in the pool with light swimming for recovery and metabolic flushing

5-6

- Recreational soccer game

Wednesday—Half Day

7:45am

- Dynamic warm up

8-10

- Tennis: Set play or specific technical work. For example, attack and volley focus, or defending focus

10-1130

- Fitness: Stamina or agility focus and finish with injury prevention and stretching

1130-12

- Recovery in pool with light swimming for recovery and metabolic flushing

12-1

- Lunch

1-2pm

- Recreational soccer game

Thursday

7:45am

- Dynamic warm up

8-10

- Tennis training: Drills and skill development. Volley and overhead training

- Forehand attack training. Basket focus and some live ball drills

10-1130

- Physical conditioning: Circuit strength training routine

1130-12

- Static stretching

12-1

- Lunch

1-230pm

- Tennis: Typically live ball points and set play. Strategy

230-4

- Fitness with a mobility, stability and flexibility focus
- Core work and lower back
- Scapular mobility
- Hip mobility
- Static stretching

4-430

- Light swimming in pool for recovery and metabolic flushing

5-6

- Recreational soccer game

Friday

7:45am

- Dynamic warm up

8-10am

- Tennis training: Drills and skill development. Weapon building focus. Basket focus and some live ball exercises

10-1130

- Physical conditioning: Speed and agility training. Coordination training. Titrated if tournament ahead on weekend

1130-12

- Static stretching

12-1

- Lunch

1-230pm

- Tennis: Typically live ball points and set play. Tactical focus

230-4

- Stamina training distance run. Yoga or stretching and mobility. No running if tournament on Saturday

4-430

- Recovery in the pool. Light swimming for metabolic flushing

5pm

- Recreational soccer game

Saturday—Half Day

7:45am

- Dynamic warm up

8-10

- Tennis: Set play or specific technical work

10-1130

- Fitness: Stamina or agility focus and finish within jury prevention and stretching

1130-12

- Recovery in the pool with light swimming for metabolic flushing

12-1

- Lunch

1pm

- Recreational soccer game

Sunday—Rest Day

- Recovery. Often swimming in the pool or at the beach. Soccer might be played on Sunday too

The conditioning and physical training work is the glue that holds the Spanish game together. Without great physical condition, the Spanish game style fails—errors creep into the shots, players lose focus and patience, and they cannot finish a long, tough match. As sports psychologist Dr. Jim Loehr likes to say, "You cannot be mentally tough without being physically fit. You simply cannot play the Spanish way without being a physical beast. All players, coaches, and parents can benefit from the Spanish focus on conditioning, stamina, injury prevention, and of course, racquet speed development (arm speed). Injury prevention is an area that is not focused on nearly enough in many areas around the world.

Regular musculoskeletal injury prevention screenings and a professional prehab program are also critical to player health and success because an injured player cannot hoist the trophy! Stamina work is important as a base for all players regardless of game style, although more conservative defensive players may need to prioritize this area more. Developing racquet and arm speed is vital for all players regardless of game style. Acceleration training on the court, as detailed in Chapter 2, can be complemented and enhanced with off-court power training in the gym. Add these Spanish *hig three*—injury prevention, stamina work and acceleration training—to your training program to benefit from this secret of Spanish success.

CHAPTER 6

Suffering

"In order for a player to play well he or she needs to suffer"
—Pato Alvarez

Spanish players love to suffer. If they come out of the court with clay on their shoes, their socks, even if they fell—it's even better. They're happy."
—Pedro Rico

"Over the course of my career I learned to love to suffer."
—Rafael Nadal

After visiting academy after academy, and interviewing coach after coach, I was astounded at how one after another stressed the same principle: suffering. Suffering to the Spanish means mental toughness, perseverance, and a fighting spirit. It is part of the tennis culture and every young Spanish player is expected to learn to fight and suffer on the red clay—to never give up.

Rafael Nadal demonstrates this mental strength perhaps better than any other professional player. Sometimes it seems Nadal likes to suffer! David Ferrer also loves to suffer. Alcaraz has the same mentality. All the Spanish players are warriors in this mold and are taught to be fighters who never give up on the court. If a Spanish guy is your opponent, you may be bigger, stronger, or more powerful, but you know you are in for a dogfight and that the Spaniard will not tank or give in. Whether in practice or in a match, the same willingness to suffer is demanded by Spanish coaches of their players.

Said Albert Costa, 2002 French Open champion and now a top coach, "What I'm trying to do is make them think that every day they have to do something else. If they go to the edge one day, the next day they have to go a bit farther. Every day they have to go farther. When I was a player, I was a fighter. I know I had good quality tennis, but when I was practicing I was always going to the edge. Every day that you step up in the court, you have to do something else, or try to improve something." Going to the edge is a hallmark of Spanish training. Practices are designed to be very demanding. Toni Nadal uses the word "exigent," or *demanding*, frequently. Toni says that a good coach must be kind and caring but also very exigent—very demanding. Demanding for Toni means always pushing hard the way Albert Costa is describing, and Toni definitely pushed his nephew Rafa this way since he was a kid—with incredible results—22 major singles titles.

Toni and Rafa Nadal frequently talk about the word "endurance" and the importance of being able to *endure*. Endurance for them is not just the concept of stamina, but the psychological qualities of perseverance and a willingness to suffer. Toni's method of building character will be discussed more in Chapter 8, but suffice it to say that suffering and endurance are a major pillars in his coaching system. Antonio Cascales, whose method and influence are presented in Chapter 9, has a similar mentality to Toni Nadal. Cascales, who along with his former student Juan Carlos Ferrero, have overseen the development of Carlos Alcaraz for many years at the Ferrero Tennis Academy. Alcaraz was taught the value of hard work and suffering since he was a teenager training at the academy.

Importantly, Spanish players are taught to be fighters but also to be humble sportsmen or sportswomen. There is beauty in the toughness yet humility and integrity that typifies the Spanish mentality of Jose Higueras, for example, who was himself an incredible fighter on the court. Higueras has told the author, in a personal interview, that he believes the willingness to suffer and fight is one of the key elements missing in American juniors. In fact, the USTA has been sending squads of elite American players over to Barcelona Total Tennis for many years now to learn how to train—and more importantly, suffer the Spanish way. Toni Nadal—currently one of the most famous, influential, and powerful figures in Spanish tennis—is one of many coaches who places humility as one of the highest values to develop in a player. He preached humility to Rafa incessantly. Toni says, "Humility means I understand that the world will go on without me," and "that the world is quite big enough without me." Antonio Cascales transmits a similar message to his students, insisting that they know their place and stay humble. Carlos Alcaraz and Rafael Nadal are paragons of the humble Spanish champion: willing to suffer to the end and humble no matter how much success they achieve. The message that the player is not bigger than the world and that the player must check his or her ego is constantly taught to the tennis players in Spain. Somehow, the country has systematized character building virtues of hard work, suffering, and humility—not an easy feat!

When Spanish coaches said to me quite earnestly, "We teach the players how to suffer," I first wondered if they were serious. It was a shock for me to hear those words said everywhere when the typical American mindset is to often cater to the player and try to make the player comfortable. Making a player comfortable and happy is a philosophy found in many clubs in the United States and especially at country clubs. My old coach Gilad Bloom, a tough Israeli who understood the importance of suffering, used to criticize this "country club mentality in the United States." Time after time, I would hear different coaches from different clubs around Spain echo the same sentiments about suffering—and the message became clear to me: Suffering is simply a way of life for the Spanish-trained tennis player.

The Spanish are deadly serious about training hard and setting up exercises to develop a player's courage and fighting spirit. Lluis Bruguera's philosophy perfectly encapsulates the messaging I heard all across Spain: "If a player isn't willing to suffer, to sacrifice, it's impossible to win." When I asked him how he goes about achieving this with players at his former academy, he told me, "We force them." Bruguera suggested spending 4-5 hours (on and off the court) daily with your players pushing them physically and mentally. Bruguera recommended a lot of drills: "More, more, more. That's more difficult for the coach and player, but the result at the end is better."

Lluis also admitted to the author in a personal interview that he didn't believe it was possible to develop a champion without tough basket drilling. The long, classic Spanish drills, with repetitions of 20-60 balls or more—nonstop—are one of the classic ways that Spanish coaches force players to learn discipline and to never give up. There is nothing like hitting your 30th ball—legs burning, lungs on fire—only to realize that you still have 30 more shots left to go in the exercise! That teaches suffering better than any other drill I know. There is a reason that "sigue," *to persist, to continue, to carry on, to go on,* in Spanish, is one of the most commonly used words by coaches on the drilling court. The Spanish drills usually keep going and going, always continuing and thus forcing the player to suffer more. Spanish players are consistently taught across the country to "go one more!"

Although some elite Spanish coaches like Jofre Porta make drills tough with just 5-10 balls, it is the suffering that comes from stamina drilling of 20 or more that builds the mental toughness the Spanish coaches are looking for, and these long sets are typical in Spain. Suffering is usually trained using volume. In Spain, of course, the tough running and conditioning (as mentioned in Chapter 5) are another important way of teaching players to learn how to suffer. Distance running and hill running are two ways to really simulate the pain and suffering that occurs in a long three or five set match at the French Open. From the youngest years, players are taught through drills and physical conditioning—and through the matches they play on the slow, red clay—that a tennis match is a fight to the death, and that they must never give up, and always embrace suffering. Suffering eventually becomes a way of life for Spanish players, and they develop a tremendous grit that they can tap into during long, arduous matches.

Franco, Stoicism, the Reconquista, the Conquistador, and Suffering

I wondered if suffering came from the Spanish culture itself. I asked the coaches I met how Spanish tennis became associated with suffering. Many Spanish coaches, including Toni Nadal, have read and espouse Stoic philosophy. Stoicism, which values self-control in the face of adversity, is defined as the endurance of pain or hardship without the display of feelings or complaint. Emilio Sanchez pointedly observed that the whole country suffered for decades under Ferdinand Franco's totalitarian rule. Interestingly, the meteoric rise of Spanish tennis coincided with the end of the Franco regime, but ironically the infrastructure and ingredients for the growth of tennis in the country were developed by Franco himself and his obsession with tennis for the Spanish people. Franco's oppression may have hardened the public and made them capable of enduring high levels of suffering while he simultaneously spread the game around the country. When Franco died, the newly liberated democratic people developed a love for tennis and were willing to suffer on the court for athletic greatness. Eventually Spain dominated the world tennis scene, propelled by the passion and perseverance of the athletes themselves and two dynamic coaches: Pato Álvarez and Lluis Bruguera.

The theme of suffering is also a core part of the dominant catholic tradition and religion in Spain. For example, a friend of mine referenced the artwork of the Spanish painter Goya, who depicted suffering as a constant theme in his work, so perhaps there was some cultural connection and deeper historical underpinning to this masochistic philosophy? I asked Ryan Schmitz, PhD, professor of Spanish at Texas Christian University. Says Schmitz, "There is a historical connection with modern day Spanish tennis players and the influence of the warrior figure from 711-1492 during the Christian Reconquest as well as the figure of the *Conquistador* in the New World, specifically with the personality traits and moral codes that this entailed. I see many of these traits in Nadal and Alcaraz (respect for the rival, the rules, and the game while simultaneously being absolutely ferocious competitors willing to do anything to win; a willingness to suffer; and a level of determination and force of will power that few humans attain." It seems apparent that the rise of Spanish tennis and the character traits of Spanish tennis champions are linked to recent Spanish history vis-a-vis Franco, and they also have deeper historical links with the Christian reconquest and the conquistador ethos and moral codes.

The love of suffering is the best and simplest way to describe how Spanish players approach tennis and aspire to be the most mentally tough fighters in the tournament. When I asked Pedro Rico (former coach of Spanish player Carlos Boluda) about Spanish players being more willing to suffer, he said, "No, they are not willing to suffer. They *love* to suffer. If they come out of the court with clay on their shoes, their socks, even if they fell—it's even better. They're happy."

Drills to Learn How to Suffer:

Pato's Famous Three Zones Drill

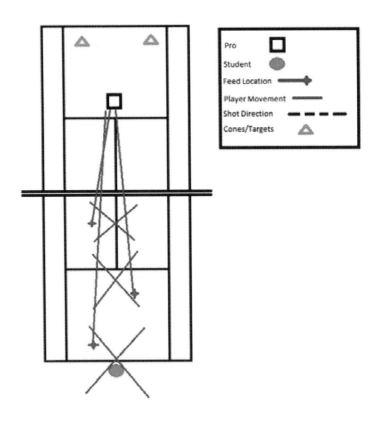

Purpose: To develop the capacity to suffer and endure through extremely long sequences of shots while moving through all three zones of the court—baseline, midcourt, and net—following the predescribed patterns in the Pato Alvarez method. The drills also helps to develop good footwork and—

from a tactical perspective defense, offense, and finishing at the net

Key Details:

- The player must follow the X pattern through the baseline, midcourt, and frontcourt at the net. Pato linked these three zones together using X patterns to create a combined super drill

- Good balance and positioning to receive the ball "between the hip and shoulder" at the optimal contact point

- Racquet acceleration on every swing

- The coach should try to keep a steady feeding rhythm, not too fast and not too slow, grinding the player down through attrition

- The player should not walk and should try to achieve the optimal position to receive every ball

- *Siempre Sigue*. Always continue. Always go one more! *Sin Cesar*. Never stop

- Racquet fed from across the net by the coach

Repetitions: 100 or more balls consecutively. The coach can adjust the repetitions based on the player's skill and fitness level

Pato's Famous Three Buckets/Baskets

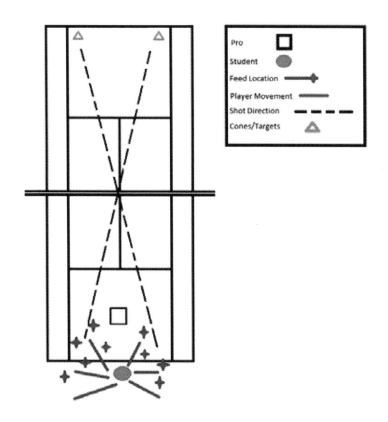

Pro   ☐

Student   ⬤

Feed Location

Player Movement

Shot Direction

Cones/Targets   △

Purpose: Pato's three basket drill is another famous exercise that he used to break a player down mentally and physically. In Spain, buckets are traditionally used to hold balls rather than carts. These buckets are called *cubos*, and Pato would continuously feed balls from each bucket until the player collapsed or finished all the balls. The purpose is to physically and mentally exhaust the player, teach him or her to suffer well, and develop technical and footwork discipline in the face of extreme adversity

Key Details:

- The player must hit the ball wherever the coach feeds it, typically in situations around the baseline on offense and defense

- Good balance and positioning to receive the ball "between the hips and shoulders" at the optimal contact point

- Racquet acceleration on every swing

- The coach should try to keep a steady feeding rhythm, not too fast and not too slow, grinding the player down through attrition

- The player should not walk and should try to achieve the optimal position to receive every ball

- *Siempre Sigue.* Always continue. Always go one more! *Sin Cesar.* Never stop

- The coach hand feeds or taps the ball up softly with the racquet from the same side of the net as the player

Repetitions: The goal is three total *cubos* or buckets consecutively, typically 240 balls more or less (80 balls per bucket). The coach can adjust the repetitions based on the player's skill and fitness level. For example, a half bucket, full bucket, or two buckets could be a goal

Classic Cross Court and Down

The Line Grinding

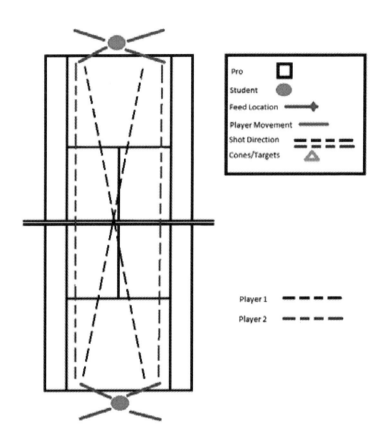

Purpose: To make the player suffer both physically and mentally while working on movement and control of the ball

Key Details:

- Live ball patterns where two players grind baseline shots

- There are many variations and patterns such as one player hits crosscourt while the other plays down the line, one ball for each player. Two shots for each player or three shots for each player before changing direction are other options. One player can change direction while the other always plays cross or down the line. One player can slice while the other plays topspin. One player can invert the forehand while the other does not

- The players must both work hard with the feet, achieving good balance and positioning to receive the ball "between the hips and shoulders" at the optimal contact point

- Racquet acceleration on every swing. No pushing allowed

- No Mistakes!

- The players must both chase every ball and be willing to suffer

- The players should try to make good tactical decisions about the outgoing shot depending on court position and the strength of the incoming ball

Repetitions: The exercise can be for a total stroke count determined by the coach or for time. The longer the rally the better

Toni Nadal's 20 Ball Scramble

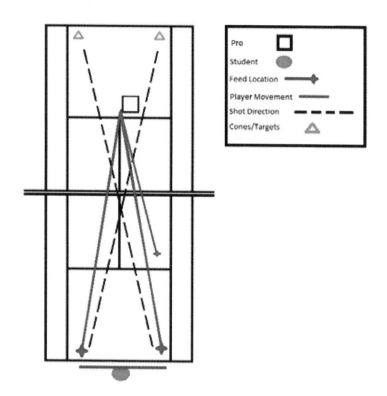

Purpose: To build discipline and make the player suffer, and to develop good reaction and quickness while taking the ball on the rise

Key Details:

- The player must hug the baseline and take the balls on the rise

- The coach feeds aggressive powerful shots—in quick succession—that the player must absorb

- The player must react quickly and prepare fast

- The player should stay low and be ready to drop down low for low fast balls

- From time to time the coach can surprise feed a more challenging wide ball or short ball or drop shot to add to the suffering

- The player must chase every feed and give maximum intensity and effort for every ball

Repetitions 20 balls

Bruguera Wall Unlimited

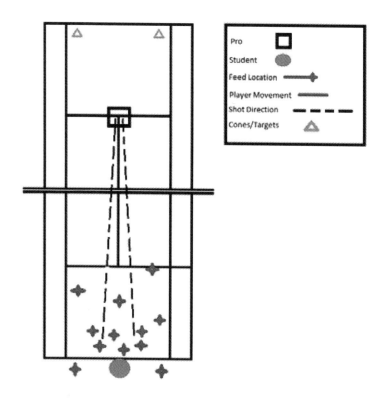

Purpose: To make the player suffer both physically and mentally. The exercise also develops concentration as the coach and player can keep one ball going together for an unlimited amount of time. Sometimes this drill can exceed 20-30 minutes length with only one ball—so it can be extreme! Garbine Muguruza, according to the coaches at Bruguera Academy, once hit 840 balls in a row!

Key Details:

- The player hits rally shots to the coach's chest or midsection

- The coach volleys softly, floating the ball back to the player. The coach's volley should move the player gently forward and backward, or left and right, at the coach's discretion

- The player must work hard with the feet, achieving good balance and positioning to receive the ball "between the hips and shoulders" at the optimal contact point

- Racquet acceleration on every swing. No pushing allowed

- No Mistakes!

- No quit!

Repetitions: Unlimited. The drill continues until either the player misses or the coach misses a volley

Examples Of Off-Court Suffering

- Mountain circuits. Hill running. Hill sprints. Hill intervals, etc.
- Stair running
- Running long distances five miles or more
- High-intensity interval training (HIIT)

Coaches, parents, and players can learn from the Spanish way of teaching players to suffer both on court and off court. Most importantly, understanding that stamina training has tremendous value and should be used to develop mental toughness and concentration, not just for the more obvious physical benefits.

Endurance-type training has become out of style in recent years with trainers continuing to stress more short sprint work to mimic the ratio of rest/work in a typical tennis match. Trainers argue that too much endurance work may actually make players slower—actually developing more slow-twitch fibers in the muscles. Recent sport science studies have demonstrated that muscle fiber types are indeed malleable to an extent, but also that the plasticity of fast-twitch versus slow-twitch fibers is more complicated than simply stating that slow running makes an athlete slow. Genetics play a large role in the amount of fiber types and their plasticity, for example, and fiber changes that do occur are typically small and have not been proven permanent in some cases. Scientists are still debating how much fiber types can change and how permanent or reversible those changes are, whether some muscle groups are more plastic than others, whether fiber type changes vary at different ages, and even the mechanisms that account for any changes. There are a lot of scientific questions still to be answered on the subject. What can be said with certainty is that years of successful Spanish endurance training suggest the fear of running a tennis athlete to the point of making him or her slow is probably overdone. The training in Spain has demonstrated that longer duration drilling and distance running are still a valuable means of training players, both for the physical and particularly for the mental benefits.

Suffering is an important component of the Spanish values system. Coaches, parents, and players can work to develop a strong character by building the capacity to suffer along with these other core psychological components of the Spanish method:

- Discipline

- Perseverance

- Fighting Spirit

- Concentration

- Pain Tolerance

- Sportsmanship—respect for others, and teamwork

- No Excuses

The character building approach in Spain incorporates suffering and the values above. Toni Nadal is probably the most famous coach in Spain to demonstrate and practice his character developing principles. His philosophy is detailed in Chapter 8.

*Part II:

The Legendary Coaches, Players

and Academies*

CHAPTER 7

The Coaching Legends and Their Legacy

While I hesitate to call Lluis Bruguera and Pato Alvarez the founding fathers of Spanish tennis—and Lluis has specifically asked me not to use that language to describe his influence—after years of interviews and research, it became clear to me that these two coaches were instrumental in developing the system of training in Spain that lead to the rise of the Spanish Armada in the late 1980s and 1990s, and that they had a profound influence on the coaching education system in Spain.

Lluis and Pato were the oldest generation of coaches in Spain that I interviewed and the pioneer private coaches in the country, who both left the national federation in the 1970s to strike out on their own and to develop top players privately. It is not a coincidence that Spain went from a decent developer of clay court players to a world superpower internationally at the same time these two genius coaches went out on their own and began a new way of teaching talented Spanish junior players. When their players started to have great success both in Spain and internationally, they received a tremendous amount of attention from the coaching community in Spain, especially the up-and-coming coaching generation. The contemporaries of Lluis and Pato and especially younger coaches wanted to learn the methods that were finally consistently producing great Spanish players. Toni Nadal, Antonio Cascales, and Jofre Porta, who are discussed in subsequent chapters, were all influenced by the philosophy and methodology of Lluis and Pato.

The federation did not turn a blind eye either, and the Spanish tennis federation's national coaching curriculum was undoubtedly influenced by the methods of Pato and Lluis. Thus a country-wide style of training was created and the imprint of these great coaching minds became readily seen across all the different clubs, from the north of the country to the south, from the east to the west.

Remember that Spain is a fairly moderate sized country – with about 30 million people in 1960 and about 47 million people estimated in 2014. To have two genius coaches tirelessly working in the country, developing not only the top playing talent, but also sharing their system with the younger generations of coaches, was a key part of Spanish success.

Pato and Lluis dramatically reshaped the system in Spain, and because of Spain's generational focus, that created a momentum that the younger generation of coaches, from Jose Perlas to Emilio Sánchez and many others have continued today. Many of the leading coaches in Spain are recognized in Chapter 11.

Lluis Bruguera

Lluis Bruguera is a creative, intelligent, charismatic and passionate coach, who founded the Bruguera Top Team Academy in Barcelona, an academy with a leading reputation in Europe that unfortunately now has closed. Lluis currently has a new project in Barcelona as adviser to Bardou Tennis Academy. Lluis has developed over 15 top 100 ATP players and notably, Garbine

Lluis Bruguera

Muguruza, a former world No. 1 WTA player. Bruguera has extensive experience coaching both juniors and professional level players. He is perhaps best known as the father and coach of Sergi Bruguera, two-time French Open champion in 1993 and 1994, who reached No. 3 in the world.

Sergi's rise to prominence catapulted Lluis to the top of the coaching world in Spain, and he was able to influence countless other Spanish coaches who wanted to learn his methods and training techniques. Therefore, the role Lluis has played in Spain's rise to international dominance cannot be underestimated. Bruguera has worked hard developing a system he feels can help a player go from "good" to pro. In a private interview Lluis said, "The United States: 20 million players. Spain: 115,000 tennis players—not young, in total. And we have more than 15 top 100s. It's incredible—15%

in the world. And every year, you see, two more. That means the system works."

Lluis Bruguera and Pato Alvarez (profiled below) were the most important coaching influences in the 1970s and 1980s that helped propel Spain to a new level of success on the world tour. Albert Costa said they were the first to pioneer the movement toward private academies and private coaching. "They started to travel with the players, that was the difference. In the clubs, we had always trainers, but not coaches. From that point I think everybody sees that we can create a private academy, we can travel with the players."

Lluis currently oversees the training at Bardou Tennis Academy in Barcelona, and he is also focused on bringing his Spanish method to Asia. Lluis's philosophy is fairly straightforward. He believes in hard work and having a good, positive attitude. His players train 3-3.5 hours a day on the court and two hours physical conditioning, and Lluis is very adamant about avoiding overtraining by keeping players fresh and hungry for more tennis each week.

Lluis was one of the first Spanish coaches to come up with a training formula that emphasizes physical conditioning almost as much as tennis training. In Lluis's training model, the extra athletic conditioning per week (double what most academies perform) and the reduced court time help players avoid overtraining and overuse injuries. He believes in a holistic approach to training, where all aspects of a player's life are guided so as to ensure success—technical, tactical, physical, and mental skills are all covered in a balanced manner.

Lluis is an expert on the psychology of tennis players and even sometimes lectures on psychology at a local university sports program in Barcelona. Fernando Luna, one of Lluis's protégés, has praised Bruguera for his great motivation techniques. "He is a very good psychologist," Luna said. "He believes every time you can win. He transmits this to you." He also "pushes a lot... and this is very, very important."

Some of the drills from Lluis have been discussed in previous chapters. Indeed, many of the classic Bruguera drills have become used so often in Spain that they are now known simply as "Spanish" drills. Lluis believes that the most important aspect that young players need to develop is the "competitive spirit." Like many Spanish coaches, Lluis's technical parameters of acceptability are very broad, and he prefers not to change grips and swings "if the player is playing very well with those shots."

In Bruguera's system, most of the technical work involves developing racquet speed, footwork and fine tuning, rather than making any major changes. "For me," he says, "the power (of the body) is not important. It's the speed (of the racquet!)." Technically, Lluis is most concerned with the action of the hand and racquet at the contact zone; the rest of the swing is not as much of a priority for him. He insists the game of tennis is simple to learn. The game is "facile," he says. At the contact zone, Lluis wants good extension of the racquet and arm—through the ball and out to the target. Lluis calls this "hitting through the line of the shot," and, of course, Luis desires massive whip and racquet speed. If you have ever watched Lluis's son Sergi play, you can tell that Lluis knows how to develop racquet speed. Sergi was not a big guy, maybe six feet one inch tall and skinny, but he could surely hit a heavy ball. His forehand measured the most RPMs of any pro for years until Rafael Nadal came on the tour with his monster forehand. It is not surprising that Lluis has some excellent racquet speed drills that are used regularly in his coaching (as detailed in Chapter 2).

Another key part of his development system is what Lluis calls, "intuitive intelligence," which he believes must be developed in all his players for them to achieve maximum on-court performance. The "intuitive intelligence," for Lluis, must be unlocked by nurturing a player's natural instincts and developing the subconscious, automatic processes of a player so that in the heat of battle he or she can perform instinctively, rather than mechanically or through conscious application. It is for this reason that Bruguera favors the guided discovery and implicit forms of teaching. He believes that this style of teaching helps develop intuitive intelligence better than any other pedagogical method. He said, "When somebody like Andy Roddick is hitting the ball at you at 140 mph, you need to build the intuitive intelligence enough to hit the ball back."

"I try to build one player," he said. "And I prefer to show that player he can make everything. But I don't want to say how he needs to play. With that, you have the opportunity to grow your player. If you force your player to play only like this, it's not developing the intuitive intelligence. For that, for me, I introduced a lot of change in the system of the game."

Lluis believes that groundstroke consistency is the key to developing a top player. He was one of the first coaches, along with Pato, to extend drills to even longer repetitions per set, such as 20 or more balls, to improve the stamina and concentration necessary to be more consistent. He says that without a good, consistent baseline game, players will not have the confidence to play at a high level or maximize their performance. Poor consistency, in his view, leads to eventual anxiety on the court.

As is typical all across Spain, the baseline groundstroke development is at the heart of the curriculum in the Bruguera method. Having personally studied with Lluis for many years, I was most impressed by his motivational abilities. Lluis is a master motivator, like many other great coaches, and he is a great communicator with his students. Lluis says that "inspiration" is one of the most important things a coach can give his students. Giving players motivation and self-belief through inspiration and good communication is something Lluis Bruguera values highly and performs exquisitely well: "My method is don't talk and don't think," he said. "Do it and be automatic. That means intuitive intelligence. Also be positive. Don't say never, no. Also it's important to give time to the players to find the way. Because even if you think that it's easy and it's very obvious what you want and what they need to do, you need to give time for 'try.'"

The Simple Method of Lluis Bruguera—10 Keys

"Tennis is simple, facile—yet most coaches complicate everything," says Lluis Bruguera. Indeed, in this era of technological advancement and scientific achievement, there is an unprecedented amount of information available about the game of tennis. We have tremendous tools as coaches, from racquet sensors and smart courts, video analysis and online resources, to name a few. For modern coaches, parents and players, sifting through this vast data can be laborious and confusing, to say the least. It can be difficult to know how to practice and design a successful blueprint to develop a champion player.

The Bruguera method shows that a simple, clear-minded approach can be successful in this complex age of information. With a relatively spartan philosophy and training system, Lluis has been incredibly successful. Here are ten tenets of the Bruguera approach that players, coaches, and parents can all learn from:

1. Train on clay when children are young to help develop patience, strategy, stamina, racquet speed, and footwork and balance. Use hard courts to develop attacking skills and quick reactions as players grow older.

2. Don't talk too much to students and don't over-analyze. Find the right exercise for the individual and let players discover the answer rather than tell them everything. Lluis commonly says, "Coaches always want to tell a student what they know. It's better to find the right exercise and let the player figure out the answer. And for this, the coach must give the player time for trial and error."

3. Be positive with children. Lluis says, "Never say 'No.' Never tell a player he can't!" Don't be overly negative or critical. Inspire and foster each player's dream with positive reinforcement. Be tough and disciplined but without being verbally abusive. Never squash a child's big dream.

4. Be solid. For Bruguera, this means consistency. Spanish players are known for this quality. Lluis says, "To be solid, to be

consistent, this does not mean you are a defensive player." He also adds, "To be solid, to know that you can put the ball inside the lines every time, this builds mental confidence and reduces the anxiety of the player."

5. Develop decision-making skills and remember that there is no perfect technique. In the Bruguera approach—and all across Spain—the focus is on the tactical decision-making of the player and control of the ball, rather than on developing perfect form according to some abstract model. This saves development time and allows for player individuality and creativity. Spanish coaches like Bruguera build smart tactical players with broad technical parameters rather than with very specific technical prescriptions.

6. Focus on footwork, movement and balance. Reading the incoming ball with the eyes and positioning the body well to receive the ball is an obsession in Spain, and this is the focus in the Bruguera style as well. Instead of obsessing about technical form, Bruguera obsesses about the balance and body control of the player when receiving and sending the ball.

7. Use topspin and develop a big forehand weapon. In the Bruguera method, the forehand with massive topspin is a primary method of attack. Bruguera uses a series of special exercises to develop the whippy style of forehand made famous by his son, Sergi. But Lluis is flexible. Some players cannot develop heavy spin and must hit flatter. If you look at Muguruza's style, you can see she plays flatter than traditional Spanish players.

8. Tennis—at its core—is a game of errors. Bruguera constantly reinforces to players that the essence of the game is to make fewer errors than the opponent. Winners and weapons are important, but making fewer errors is more important. This message is especially important for young, developing players to learn before they grow into their bodies and develop power. It's also an important message for less talented players and players prone to anxiety.

9. Don't overtrain. Play less tennis and do more physical work off the court to build endurance, become a better athlete, and to stay healthy. Injured players don't win tournaments, don't move up the rankings, and don't get a paycheck. Lluis always says, "It's better to stop when a player still wants to play more, so he is hungry to come back the next morning." Lluis also contends that, "players with better physical conditioning make smarter decisions over the course of a match."

10. Teach players that tennis—and life—involves suffering. For Bruguera, tennis is a game of sacrifice, discipline, and physical and mental suffering. The player who is willing to suffer the most on the court generally wins in the end. This is especially true for players who want to one day win a clay court tournament like Roland Garros, where endurance is critical to success.

Lluis has proved that with his simple approach, hard work, and a willingness to suffer, champions can be developed in a very efficient and practical way, even in today's modern world of big data, scientific development, and technological advancement.

Former student and top 30 ATP player Fernando Luna said, "Lluis Bruguera was my coach for many years. I learned from him many, many good things. I think Lluis is the best coach in the world, for many years. When I finished my career, I started to work with him as a coach."

Consistency, positive attitude, racquet speed development, movement and balance, work ethic, athletic development, technical and tactical automation, and inspiration: these are some of the core elements of Lluis's philosophy and system. Combine that with a coach who is passionate and committed to the excellence of his students and to their holistic development, and you have the makings of a super coach who has influenced the trajectory of Spanish tennis immeasurably.

Visit the Chris Lewit YouTube channel and book website for exclusive, unedited interviews with Lluis about his influence on Spanish tennis, philosophy, and training methods.

Pato Alvarez

"I consider myself the best coach due to the results I have achieved with my players; it's not because I am more able than anyone else. Simply, for them, tennis is work, while for me tennis is my entire life."
—William Pato Alvarez

William "Pato" Alvarez was one of the legendary coaches in Spain, who, along with Lluis Bruguera, was instrumental in dramatically changing the training system in that country, paving the way for the "Spanish Armada," as the rising Spanish tennis players of that era were called. He was very influential in developing the protocols that many future Spanish coaches would follow, now known as "The Spanish Way."

Pato ("duck" in Spanish), originally from South America, came to Spain after having had a world-class career, competitive with the top players on the professional tour at that time ("Top 10," he said, although there were no official top 10 rankings at that time). He played in all the grand slams and competed against the best players of his era. After his playing career ended, he was working for years with the Spanish Federation's top players in the 1970s, and then became one of the first private coaches in Spain along with Lluis Bruguera and Ion Tiriac.

William "Pato" Alvarez

Over the long span of his career, Pato, also known as "panther" to his players, developed dozens of top professional Spanish competitors such as Emilio Sánchez and Sergio Casal. He specialized in taking teenage players ages 15 and up and preparing them for the transition to the professional ranks. More recently, Pato was working with Grigor Dimitrov and he was traveling and coaching with Andy Murray—both during their teenage years. On the tour, Pato's players were called "little ducks" and included, at different times, Emilio Sánchez, Sergio Casal, Pato Clavet, Tomás Carbonell, Javier Sánchez, Jordi Burillo, Joan Balcells, Julián Alonso, Carlos Cuadrado and Joan Albert Viloca, among others. His group rivaled the group of Luis

Bruguera, whose original tour proteges included Joan Aguilera, Fernando Luna, Jordi Arrese, and Sergi Bruguera.

Pato designed the system of drills that is now being used at Emilio Sánchez Academy, one of the leading academies in Spain and the world, and was based at ESA and taught lessons when he was not traveling with his charges to tournaments. I have had the privilege to study with Pato on the court and observe him. He was a very intelligent, funny, charismatic, and affable coach.

He seemed playful and eccentric, but there was a twinkle in his eye when he spoke that revealed someone to be taken seriously with unique knowledge to share—perhaps the very secrets of Spanish tennis. Sergio Casal, former ATP player and one of Pato's star students, explained that before Pato nobody in Spain drilled seriously from the basket. Pato created this extensive sequence of drills to work all technical/tactical areas and linked them together into a comprehensive system of training. Said Casal, "What we try to teach with this system is: get better with every area of the court." Pato used these drills to teach his students how to suffer for many decades! He worked his players at a very high intensity until some of them would crawl off the court from fatigue.

Pato was known as being one of the toughest coaches because of his reputation for exhausting players during training sessions. Some of Pato's drills have been featured earlier in this book, and many more are explained in his book *El Guru del Tenis*. I believe that I have the only English-translated copy of Pato's book in the world. Pato created hundreds of exercises over his career, but only a select few became his favorites and the ones he recommended for the daily work of the player.

Players who visit the Emilio Sánchez Academy in Barcelona will be doing many of the exercises that Pato designed and used to take Spanish pros to the top of the game.

10 Tennis Truths According To Pato:

Pato Alvarez had a unique philosophy about how to play the game of tennis. He created a list of hundreds of tennis truths that he called the "Patology." Here are 10 principles from his book El Guru del Tenis that help explain his perception of the game and his vision for how to develop world-class tennis players:

1. The born tennis champion needs to have a minimum of three things: a head, a heart, and legs. The ideal percentage for me is 60 percent head, 20 percent heart, and 20 percent legs.

2. The "double rhythm," which is the game of the feet that I invented, consists basically of giving two side steps forwards or backwards, in a way that you always arrive well placed to hit the ball in front of your body.

3. In tennis, if you always play with the same rivals, you will stay at their same level.

4. To play tennis at a high level you need four important things: good training against strong players, a high level of competition, competent coaching, and money to pay for all these expenses.

5. Tennis is a game of errors. He who commits fewer errors generally wins. Between the necessary virtues to be a good player, the most important is to be capable of giving away very little points by errors. The majority of players try to play pretty and strong, and that is all well and good, but only if they commit little errors.

6. In tennis, true champions are those who can endure the pressure and always play the important points well, either because they never give gifts of errors, or because they make you beat them.

7. A player who is tired can hardly think on a tennis court. A player in very good shape thinks more clearly than another with the same ability but who is in worse shape.

8. Unless you have a better backhand than forehand, you should cover three-fourths of the backcourt with your forehand. You will dominate more of the points this way.

9. In tennis, one should always try to take fewer steps than the opponent.

10. In tennis, short distances are as good as long distances; you don't have to be obsessed with hitting hard into the corners all the time. Drop shots, angles, lobs, balls in the middle, slices and off-pace shots...they can be just as useful as strong shots to the corners.

Pato left a closing message in his book for children:

If there is something in your life that excites you and is your passion, make it your profession. If you work hard you will have success--don't doubt it. I have done the same and it has not gone badly for me. For the forgetful, here's this: Has there ever existed another coach who had four players in the top thirty of the world at the same time? I had Emilio Sanchez ranked number 7 in the world, Javier Sanchez at 20, Francisco Clavet at 24, and Sergio Casal at 30, all at the same time, in addition to having the doubles pair Sanchez-Casal in the top 5 in the world. This was never achieved on the ATP circuit before, and I'm willing to dare to say it will never happen again!

Pato tended to work with older players who already had good technique, but when he did work on technique, he focused on footwork, balance, and—of course—generating maximum racquet speed. In fact, these areas have become the de facto skills for all Spanish players to develop. Alvarez was an extremely hard worker and coached almost every day before he passed away in 2022. Pato was working on being nominated to the Tennis Hall of Fame in Newport, RI, before his death. He was certainly one of the best coaches ever to work in Spain, and he was a leading coach on the world stage. He certainly deserves to receive recognition for his tireless efforts and dedication towards developing top professional players. As Emilio Sánchez said, "Goodbye (William Pato Alvarez), you marked my life since I was young, you helped me find my best self, you taught me to have a passion for competing, to give my best without looking around. You leave a very important legacy in the world of tennis..."

Lluis and Pato and the Six Secrets

Although historically there has been some personal conflict—and competition—between Bruguera and Alvarez, together they have had a profound influence on the trajectory of Spanish tennis and have been instrumental in shaping the Spanish style, philosophy, and methods that are being used across the country by thousands of coaches. While their methods and philosophies are different—they are also similar in many ways. In this book I have tried to highlight those similarities to give coaches, players, and parents a practical guide that is not rooted in one coach's particular dogma only. The six secrets are the result of this search for universality and harmony between the different teaching lineages in Spain. For example, Alvarez is a passionate proponent of using the double rhythm footwork as much as possible, and he makes it a primary part of his technical work. However, it would be wrong to focus primarily on the double rhythm technique and label it "The Spanish Way" because there are many other elite coaches in Spain, including Bruguera, who do not stress the double rhythm and still have achieved fantastic results.

In the six secrets of Spanish tennis in this book, I have tried to outline more broad commonalities that the great coaches in Spain would have trouble disagreeing with each other about. Pato and Lluis, despite their philosophical differences on some areas of the tennis game, would agree on the importance of training these six core fundamentals:

- Movement, footwork and balance

- Racquet speed and weapon building

- Consistency

- Defense

- Physical conditioning

- Suffering

As I have mentioned in the "Secrets" section of the book, many of these areas can be taught in an integrated way, rather than separately piece by piece. Indeed, as Luis Mediero, a leading Spanish coaching educator, has asserted, one hallmark of the Spanish approach is to teach elements simply and holistically, which is the preferred method of both Pato and Lluis. The exercises that they designed work the technical, tactical, physical, and mental, often all together. However, the drills often have the versatility to allow the coach to prioritize the areas that are the most vital for the student.

Coaches, parents, and players can feel confident adding these core Spanish elements to their own training regimens because they are endorsed by the two greatest coaches Spain has ever had, Lluis and Pato. There are other unique methods that individual Spanish coaches teach, and more specialized and varied approaches from academy to academy and coach to coach, but the purpose of this book is to highlight common themes to get to the essence of the Spanish way. However, to study the differences between coaches across Spain is a fascinating exercise.

For the curious reader, I will be adding to the book website and the Chris Lewit YouTube channel exclusive interviews with other leading Spanish coaches that I have interviewed, such as Pancho Alvarino, Antonio Martinez, Jose Altur, Jofre Porta, Albert Costa, Sergio Casal, Emilio Sánchez, Andres Gimeno, Jose Perlas, Javier Piles, Jordi Vilaró, Javier Duarte, Francis Roig, Alvaro Margets and more. Many of these greats will also be discussed in Chapter 11. Please visit the book website, to read or listen to these interviews.

Chapter 8

Toni Nadal and His Method

Toni Nadal has become one of the most famous and recognizable coaches in Spain because of his incredible tenure helping his nephew Rafael Nadal reach the pinnacle of the pro game. Currently, Uncle Toni, as he is often affectionately called, leads the Rafa Nadal Academy in Mallorca where top 10 players like Casper Ruud and Felix Auger-Aliassime have trained. Nadal has been integral in his nephew Rafael Nadal's development and career, but to the outside world he remains an enigmatic figure. This is partly due to his reclusive and protective nature. No doubt he often presents a stern—even intimidating—face to those he doesn't know well, and the question remains: has the media really ever taken him seriously? The common at times, slightly dismissive media moniker, "Uncle Toni" belies who Toni Nadal actually is. Those who know him respect his intellect, integrity, and especially his tenacity in helping to build one of the greatest players of all time.

First, Toni is a serious student of the game. True, he values his privacy and closely guards secrets he believes have led to Rafa's incredible success, but he is also known to light up in laughter in unguarded private moments—a side of his character the world never sees.

I have spent time at the academy observing training sessions and also interviewed Toni personally in Spain to learn about his philosophy and teaching methods. His system is unique and prioritizes character development. Toni Nadal firmly believes that a player's character and morals will affect his or her growth and development on the tennis court. Toni also has a strong tactical mind and spends a lot of time working on his players' strategic mind and tactical awareness. On the technical front, Toni keeps his approach simple and often works on basic principles of movement and stroke production.

Technical and Footwork Parameters

With younger players still forming their technique and footwork, Toni stresses good balance in the lower body and "seeking" the ball, which means to see the incoming ball and go forward to it. Interestingly, moving forward to seek the ball is also a pillar in the method of another famous European coach, Italian Riccardo Piatti. He says it is very important for players to see the ball early and close the distance to the ball, and that's also how he trained Rafa when he was a kid. While moving forward is important, Toni believes in developing a good defense, similar to the philosophy of many other Spanish coaches that have been included in the book. As players get older, he believes in teaching attacking and aggressive tennis.

While the method of Toni Nadal is very aggressive-minded and forehand dominant, he firmly still believes in building a base of consistency and control, which is standard practice all across the country. Toni says, "The sign of an advanced player and the key to winning in tennis is not to miss any of the easy shots. Start with that focus." Therefore Toni's method is a hybrid of sorts, building weapons and an aggressive mindset but not forgetting the Spanish foundation of consistency that was the focus of Chapter 3. For pro players, Toni states adamantly that "to be successful in today's pro game the player must be complete with no weaknesses or deficiencies" and that the player must be able to hit winners and not just grind and defend.

Toni Nadal

Toni Nadal stresses the importance of court position to his students. While Lluis Bruguera allows his players to fade back deep behind the baseline, players at the Rafa Nadal Academy look to take the ball relatively early and defend less frequently than in some other Spanish systems. Toni's philosophy on court position is to take time away when you can and position aggressively on the baseline, similar to the approach of Jordi Vilaró and Francis Roig at Barcelona Total Tennis (BTT) and Antonio Cascales at Ferrero Tennis Academy.

It's not acceptable to be just a baseline clay court grinder or specialist. Toni Nadal's vision for his players is to be strong and versatile, with the confidence to play well on all surfaces. At the Rafa Nadal Academy they have many hard courts to balance out the traditional clay court Spanish training. When asked why they have so many hard courts at the academy, Toni answered, "Being proficient on hard courts is essential in today's pro game because most professional tennis is played on hard courts."

One of Toni's favorite technical elements to work on is "accompanying the ball," which is a phrase he uses liberally. In fact, Uncle Toni has an obsession with this concept. Accompanying the ball means to follow the ball after impact with your racquet, to extend through the impact and follow along the ball pathway towards the target. I have observed many hours of Toni Nadal coaching on the court and he loves to use this teaching cue! The genius behind the concept is that it can be just as helpful for young developing players as mature pros. Accompanying the ball leads to better power, control and depth, according to Toni, and is remarkably similar to Lluis Bruguera's approach that stresses following "the line" of the shot. In fact, Bruguera and Nadal both echo each other's concepts, words, and phrases often.

Similar to Bruguera, Toni is obsessed with the footwork, balance and positioning of his players. It's critical, according to Uncle Toni, to move well and set up with balance to receive the ball in the optimal position. Toni wants a quiet upper body during the swing and strong push with the legs. He wants so much drive with the legs that he often encourages his players to literally jump off the ground with both feet or at least leaving the ground with one foot. This teaching cue was surprising for me to learn because he is the first coach in Spain whom I have witnessed actively teaching players to jump. Bruguera and Pato Álvarez, for example, have always tended to stress staying on the ground for most shots. Toni believes that, especially on the forehand, being airborne is a way of life.

Toni is also the first coach in Spain whom I have observed frequently teaching and drilling the drop shot. The drop shot, known as *la dejada* in Spanish, is a critical shot to learn on the red clay and can even be effective, as Carlos Alcaraz has demonstrated, on fast hard and grass court surfaces. Toni has many drills to develop the drop shot tactically, and he technically focuses on the technique of the drop shot as well. In my experience traveling to study with many legends in Spain and at many top academies, Toni is the first coach to systematically teach and hone the drop shot. Other coaches in Spain, like Pato and Lluis, seem to let the shot develop more organically—it's not a core aspect of their method. By contrast, for Toni Nadal the drop shot is very important, and not merely an accessory skill.

Acceleration is important to Toni in his method, but he does not usually train the acceleration with hand fed drills like Bruguera so famously does. Instead, Nadal cleverly sets up live ball points and sets parameters to get the power on the shots that he wants. Indeed, my impression of Toni Nadal as a coach is that he is a master tactician and mental game coach and less of a technical whiz. He is brilliant with the software side of the game and not as gifted at the hardware side. To wit, he comes to the court with a vast arsenal of live ball tactical exercises and games, some of which are featured in the Secrets chapters. I have made a video course of drills and methods of Lluis, Pato, and Toni which is available online at www.CLTA.teachable.com, for those who are curious and want to learn more about Nadal's system of training and philosophy.

Toni is a no-nonsense individual who doesn't tolerate any laziness or bad habits. He believes in discipline and hard work, and he expects his charges to push themselves to the limits. He can seem intimidating with a gruff outer shell, but Toni has a big heart and a wry sense of humor. He really cares about his students and can use his quick wit to break the ice or lighten the mood when he wants. Toni Nadal, similar to Lluis Bruguera, is a laconic coach, using words sparingly and choosing his words carefully. He often likes to stand very close to his players while they are hitting or playing, and he says that this is "to make them feel his presence and connect the coach with the player more intimately." Toni says, "The most important quality for a coach is kindness, caring for the player."

Toni has a famous saying about how tennis players must be developed "like rabbits." What he means by this is that unpredictability in training is very important to stimulate more growth from the player.

Tactical Priorities

Toni is obsessed with building a powerful forehand and using the forehand more than the backhand from the back court. He has stated definitively that he believes the forehand is the most important shot in the pro game, and many of his drills and exercises focus on running around the backhand well and using the forehand to attack from the backhand corner. Toni calls this shot the "drive invertido," or the inverted drive. In the United States, we call this shot the inside-out or inside-in.

Toni says the speed of the modern game has become almost unbelievable. He says, "The game is evolving and getting faster, and in our training we must be flexible and adaptable." He continues to place great emphasis on the traditional Spanish value of moving well with quick footwork while breaking tradition in some respects. Surprisingly, Toni advocates training on faster hard courts, when most of his Spanish coaching compatriots value clay. And he's not afraid to instruct his students to attack—breaking the traditional Spanish mindset obsessed with defense. He also believes that players should own all the shots, developing a complete game with multiple ways to hurt an opponent. Toni put it this way, "When I first got on tour, there were players with flaws—now everyone can do everything!" For Toni, developmental coaches must be similarly flexible and adapt to the individual. He has no tolerance for rigid systems or dogma. He asserts, "Every player is different and there is no 'only way'."

Character Building—Toni Nadal's Six Core Values

First and foremost Toni lives by a strict moral code. "Even if the world is finished tomorrow, I do the right thing—that's values. Values affect everyone and everything in the world." In addition, his system is not only a powerful way to develop good tennis players, but it is a pathway to develop good human beings and a better society—better citizens of the world. To me, this is part of the genius of his approach and the value his principles hold for others, whether they be coaches or parents.

Toni himself has said, "It is more important to be a good person than a good player." Based on this core belief, Toni has created a six point development model for the players he oversees at the academy. Here is my interpretation of these points, based on talking to Toni and on other reading and research into his thoughts.

1. Humility

The value of humility is commonly taught in Spanish tennis. Humility can be exemplified by champions like Nadal, Carlos Moya and Juan Carlos Ferrero. "Humble is the way you have to be, period," Toni says. He continues, "Everybody should know their place in the world. The point is that the world is quite big enough already without you imagining that you're big too." Rafa himself has argued that humility is a key component to his motivation and competitiveness because his humility never allows him to overestimate an opponent and become complacent going into battle.

2. Overcoming Obstacles

Toni believes that life in general has gotten faster, and that children and sometimes parents expect instant results and gratification… quick fixes. But for Toni, the things that have the most value in life are difficult and take a long time to achieve. Thus, having the perseverance to overcome obstacles is a very important value and overcoming challenges is what helps to build a strong character.

3. Respect

"Respect for other people, for everyone irrespective of who they might be or what they might do, is the starting point of everything," Toni tells John Carlin in an interview for the book, *Rafa*. "What is not acceptable is that people who have had it all in life should behave coarsely with other people. No, the higher you are, the greater your duty to treat people with respect." Furthermore, Toni believes that if you respect others, you will be happier in life, and thus happier on the difficult journey towards becoming a champion.

4. Patience

Patience is a common value taught to players in Spain. For Toni, one must, of course, be patient on the court to develop one's strategy. Moreover though, in life, one must never become impatient on the long and difficult journey towards achieving greatness; patience is thus interlinked with persistence.

5. Tolerance

Tolerance, for Toni, is connected to the value of respect. For Toni, people in life who have a high tolerance of those around them are more respectful and peaceful, and thus happier in their life. But Toni also believes tolerance is an important character trait in champions on the court. Tolerance, in this case, means how a player handles the stress and mental/

emotional challenges of the battle. Strong players are able to tolerate more stress and pressure than weaker players. Therefore, tolerance is also interwoven with the concept of self-control, echoing stoic philosophy. Toni says, "Self-control is critical to becoming a champion. A player must control their mind, body and emotions. Without this, he cannot control the ball."

6. Fighting Spirit

For Toni, fighting spirit means being willing to "suffer." Sometimes he calls it "enduring." Toni believes champions must endure and suffer. They must fight to the end to achieve greatness. Fighting spirit means never cave in. Rafa says his uncle taught him this: "Endure, put up with whatever comes your way, learn to overcome weakness and pain, push yourself to the breaking point, but never cave in. If you don't learn that lesson, you'll never succeed as an elite athlete," said Toni.

———————

These six core values are the infrastructure around which a coach can build a champion's mind and echoing stoic philosophy, one that dominates without making excuses. Above all else, Toni says, "Champions must find solutions, not excuses. Whining and complaining never helped us win a match or championship."

Three Nadal Principles of Player Development

In addition to his model of six core values for players, Toni has also summarized his player development philosophy with the following three overarching principles: Technique, Character, and Propriety.

Technique

Technique for Toni Nadal, means developing all the skills a player needs to control the ball and to make the ball go where he or she wants. For Toni, this does not mean the strokes have to be perfect—far from it. He has always emphasized being able to put the ball where a player wants and finding the right skills for a player's personality and style—a practical approach to technical development, rather than forcing every player to achieve some abstract perfect form. Says Toni, "But what is that, technique? Is it hitting the ball very hard and with a beautiful movement but once out of every two hits, it lands outside the court? Is it to have a very good forehand, a very good serve but no backhand? No. For me, technique is about being able to place the ball wherever you want it to land no matter what shot."

Character

Character, for Toni, very simply means working relentlessly towards achieving one's goals. He states, "A well-formed character is one that has been prepared to withstand the harshness of daily effort, the will, the development of self-improvement capabilities, and, not least, the enthusiasm to do so." Character relates directly to: Overcoming Obstacles, Patience, and Fighting Spirit.

Propriety

Toni Nadal believes that propriety—respect and good manners—is critical to achieving a happy life and good performance on the court. He says, "Respect and good manners bring happiness in one's life."

The efforts of Toni Nadal with Rafa have been well documented, but his teaching method and philosophy have been more obscured over the years. This chapter has shared some insight into the approach and philosophy of the man who has had the greatest Grand Slam success with his player of any coach in Spain's history. Nadal's method interweaves the six secrets of Spanish tennis with his strict moral code. Toni's unique brilliance can be found in his character building and the strategic vision for his players. He delivers his method with an economy of words, no excuses, hard work, and a willingness to suffer.

CHAPTER 9

Antonio Cascales—The Other Toni!

You probably have never heard of Antonio Cascales, but in some ways he is truly the unsung guru of Spanish tennis. You may have heard of his proteges: Juan Carlos Ferrero, Pablo Carreno Busta, and Carlos Alcaraz, who all have trained under his watchful eye. He is not very well known outside of Spain, but his coaching record rivals many other top coaches in the country—and his story is remarkable. He is credited with for guiding Juan Carlos Ferrero to No. 1 in the world and to the 2003 Roland Garros title. Cascales coached Juan Carlos since he was about 10 years old. It's a Cinderella story of how a small town coach helped a small town player become tennis champion of the world.

Cascales is also the founder, along with Juan Carlos, of the Ferrero Tennis Academy, which has grown from a tiny club with only two courts into one of the best tennis academies in the world with over 20 courts and world class facilities.

The way Antonio tells the story, the Franco regime—near the end of his rule, which ended with his death 1975—was entranced by the success of Manolo Santana in that era. In 1965 for example, Santana helped Spain defeat the United States in Davis Cup and in that year he also reached the world No. 1 amateur ranking, propelling him to national celebrity status. According to Cascales, Franco felt that tennis would be the perfect sport for the masses in the middle class across the country. The image of tennis appealed to Franco and he and his administration sought to support the growth of tennis around the country and encourage everyone to play. Prior to this time, tennis was more of a rich family sport in Spain, reserved for the wealthy families of gilded clubs in Barcelona like the Real Club de Tennis, Club Tenis Barcino and Club Tenis de la Salut, for example.

The end result was that in the late 1960s and 1970s there was a boom of tennis clubs and many more people from a lower social stratification began to play tennis around the country at their local clubs. By Cascales' estimation, tennis clubs in Spain expanded from 50 to over 800 clubs and participation exploded! By the way, these events laid the grassroots foundation on which many future professional stars for Spain were built. Many of the children who picked up a racquet during this era became the champions of the 1980s and 1990s.

Cascales, himself, was a beneficiary of this new societal embrace of tennis. By 1979, he had become one of the best local players in the region outside of Alicante. He mainly taught himself how to play and didn't have any primary mentors. The local club asked him to start a school. He replied, "Start a school? But I don't know anything!" The club leaders insisted and that is how Cascales' coaching story began, teaching himself how to teach tennis at a little club outside of a small town called Villena. He was only 18 years old.

Cascales said he slowly taught himself how to teach through trial and error and also going to seminars and conferences. He remembers that in the 1980s and early 1990s there were many RFET (Royal Spanish Tennis Federation) workshops across the country to share the teachings of Willam Pato Alvarez and Lluis Bruguera, who were dominating the coaching scene in Spain during that era. Cascales, in a personal interview, admitted that he had learned from them and others and then developed his own philosophy and methodology that he applied to his small school.

Cascales remembers that he attended a big RFET conference in 1990 where the featured speakers were Lluis Bruguera and Pato Alvarez. Cascales recalls that Lluis and Pato had big personalities and that they clashed often and did not get along with each other. In Cascales' opinion, Alvarez's system was rigid and overly structured, allowing little flexibility to customize the method for each player. Alvarez, according to Cascales, was very strict in his approach and the student either did it his way or Pato would leave the player. Cascales believes that Lluis's approach at the time was more flexible and customizable to the player. Cascales current academy, Ferrero Tennis Academy, borrows many exercises and methods that he learned from conferences like this one.

Cascales, like Toni Nadal, was heavily impacted by the philosophy and teachings of Lluis Bruguera and Pato Alvarez during that period, as almost all Spanish coaches from that era were influenced. Pato and Lluis were so dynamic and charismatic during that time—and garnered so much attention from their coaching successes—that the Spanish Federation (RFET) in the 1980s and 1990s codified the methods of these giants into a work system and propagated that methodology around the country through courses, conventions, and certification programs.

Cascales attested that for decades the RFET courses taught these approaches and drills until collaboration with the ITF education department brought some tweaks to the coaching education program in Spain. Therefore, during a critical growth period for tennis in Spain, coaches were influenced by Lluis and Pato's personal influence and guidance, but even coaches far away from the orbit of Barcelona tennis, where Lluis and Pato were kings, like Cascales, learned many of the same drills and approaches. According to Cascales, the drills and work system introduced to the country by Pato and Lluis in the 1980s dramatically changed the trajectory of Spanish tennis and helped lead to the rise of the "Spanish Armada" of top pros in the 1990s and beyond.

In 1994, Cascales founded the Equelite Academy, which later became known as the Ferrero Tennis Academy with three students achieving very big success. Pedro Rico was a star junior and went on to a full scholarship at Pepperdine in the states. Santi Ventura became a solid ATP pro, and Juan Carlos Ferrero became No. 1 in the world and won Roland Garros in 2003. Based on those successes, Cascales and the academy grew. From very humble origins—two clay courts set in the farmlands outside Villena—the academy has developed into a world powerhouse providing elite training to top professional players and juniors. It's a remarkable achievement for a coach and program operating basically in the middle of nowhere.

Cascales reminisced that in 1994 Juan Carlos was champion in Tarbes, the world junior 14U championship, and he came to live with Cascales in Villena, at the site of the current academy. The tiny club was surrounded by farming fields, orchards and vineyards on the outskirts of town. Today that same club has over 20 courts, world-class facilities, and Juan Carlos and Antonio still live onsite and oversee the training program. The academy has grown in prestige and currently has a very strong list of top juniors and ATP players who train or have trained there including Pablo Carreno Busta, David Ferrer, Nicolas Almagro, and now the prodigy Carlos Alcaraz.

Cascales is unassuming, humble, and reserved but carries an intellectual gravitas. He's the kind of coach who quietly observes and from time to time shares an important nugget of wisdom. He doesn't speak too much on the court, but when he does speak it's with authority. His coaching follows the formula of Lluis Bruguera, who once said a coach "shouldn't speak too much, but find the right exercise." He has a commanding presence only earned from the experience of years in the trenches.

Brugura Antonio insists that the game of tennis remains relatively simple, despite scientific and technological advances. While he values research and is not afraid to evolve or resistant to change, in the end he believes the game of tennis at its core remains simple and mostly the same. That's why many of the exercises he uses like the famous Spanish X drill and La Pared ("the wall") are essentially timeless, in his opinion. Many of the exercises at the academy, Cascales admits, may be influenced by Pato and Lluis and he believes it's natural to include these exercises in his work system because "they still work and are useful."

Cascales has no dogma and no rigid system that everyone must follow. When asked what the core of his teaching philosophy is, he replied, "Hard work and docility." Docility means the player is coachable, malleable. Docility implies that the player respects the coach, listens to feedback and implements it. It's essentially the ability to learn well, which the other Toni—Toni Nadal—happens to say is the most important talent of all. Docility also implies humility, an important virtue discussed in Chapter 9, because if a player thinks he is the center or the universe, he won't take instruction well.

The capacity to work is very important for Cascales. For him, the player must be able to sacrifice everything to improve his tennis and dedicate himself or herself to the goal. He told a story of how a young Juan Carlos always delivered very high energy in his training and was superior in his work ethic. Cascales said that sometimes, even after four hours of work in a day, Juan Carlos still wanted more. He was insatiable and relentless. Cascales says that Carlos Alcaraz also has these same qualities. Cascales insists that one of the main aspects that has led to Spanish success over the years is this type of "hard work and intensity in the training." Indeed, a strong work ethic is a common driver of Spanish tennis success all across the country, and Lluis and Pato were similarly obsessed with hard work and intensity.

Cascales still oversees all the training at his academy where hard work is the focus while deemphasizing too much technique or other distracting training elements. While technique and tactics are of course important, in the end, according to Antonio, the consistent engagement, growth mindset, and good old-fashioned hard work are essential ingredients needed to build a Spanish champion. Of course, he always weaves the six Spanish secrets in one way or another into his training curriculum. Cascales is a wonderful example of a coach who found big success incorporating some of the methods of Lluis and Pato into his own work system, and he was instrumental in growing the game all across Spain. While Lluis Bruguera had great success with Sergi reaching No. 3 and Pato's student Emilio reached No. 7 in the world, Juan Carlos Ferrero, coached by Antonio, achieved the No. 1 ranking.

Chapter 10

Jofre Porta:
The Maverick Genius of Mallorca

Jofre Porta's academy is called Global Tennis and it is situated on the paradise island of Mallorca (which is about a 45 minute plane ride from Barcelona). The leader of Global, Jofre is the charismatic, silver-haired and bright-eyed tennis guru who is well respected—if not as well known—as some other legends in Spain such as Lluis Bruguera or William Pato Alvarez, or even the understated Antonio Cascales.

Jofre's passion for tennis is infectious and he has dedicated his life to developing a method of training athletes to master the game, which he calls the Global System. A renegade and free spirit, Jofre's teaching methods are creative and unconventional yet he has had incredible success, having trained many of the top juniors in Spain as well as having a loyal following of international students, especially Russians and Eastern Europeans. He is a frequent speaker around the world at International Tennis Federation educational events and enjoys sharing his knowledge and exchanging ideas with other coaches. Coach, educator, and philosopher, Jofre supports his theories with an eclectic range of sources, from classical literature to the latest sport and neurological science research.

As a coach, Jofre Porta has had the unique experience of training and assisting with the training of two No. 1 players in the world in their formative years: Carlos Moya and Rafael Nadal. Jofre started working with Carlos Moya when he was under 10 years old and guided him through his early pro career. Carlos later became the first Spanish male player to reach No. 1 in the world in 1999. With Rafa, Jofre assisted Uncle Toni and traveled with Rafael to local, regional, and international junior events. Rafa also spent a year training with Porta at Global when he was under 12.

A coach is lucky to have the opportunity to experience developing one world champion player in his or her career. It is remarkable that Jofre has trained two No. 1 players, and the experiences with Nadal and Moya have shaped and colored his philosophy and training system. Something magical happened in Mallorca to produce Moya and Nadal—two No. 1 players in the world from a small island—and Jofre was a creator of and witness to this magic.

Global Tennis is Jofre's life work and passion, and his program and academy are unique. I have visited academies all over Spain, and I've never seen anything quite like it. Jofre calls his academy a "doll house" compared to other academies. What he means by that is the scale is very small and players are known intimately, like a family. This is no factory. Jofre and his wife Afiza also live on site as well, adding to the family vibe. The academy stands in stark contrast to Rafa Nadal's large, glitzy, and commercial academy about a half hour up the road, on the eastern side of the island of Mallorca. The academy is a short fifteen minute drive from Palma, the major city on the island, near the ferry terminal and airport. The facilities are spartan and simple, with five red clay courts, a small workout area and a dorm and cafe building adjacent to the courts. There are no luxuries here like at Rafa's new academy—only serious tennis training in a boot camp style.

Porta calls his training method Global System, which describes a training approach that considers all aspects of a player's development including the technical and tactical, mental and emotional, and physical. The Global System is therefore a holistic, comprehensive approach to developing champions. Jofre is genuinely concerned about the well-being of his players, not only preparing them for high level tennis, but also for life. His dedication and passion is incredible. One day he decided that he needed to be closer to his players to give them better supervision and guidance, so he and his wife moved from their comfortable house off campus directly into a corner room in the player dorms onsite.

There is a spiral staircase from Jofre's dorm room up to his office and a roof deck. From his office and roof deck he gains a panoramic view of all the coaches working and can observe players at all times. From his roof deck, he can bark out orders to his coaches and give reminders to players. In this way, the academy is very closely monitored and Jofre knows exactly how all his players are performing daily. Sometimes actions speak louder than words and this level of coaching dedication and commitment is truly amazing and reveals Jofre's passion for his students—and for developing champions in tennis and life.

I was first introduced to Jofre's philosophy and work system at the ITF World Conference in 2009 in Valencia, Spain. Jofre is known for his intelligent, dynamic, and entertaining coach education seminars and presentations, and he did not disappoint at the conference. Prior to his presentation, I remember seeing him ride up in a motorcycle, engine revving, wearing a leather jacket. His long silver hair was wild, tousled by the wind. No other coaches made an entrance like that, and I thought to myself at the time, *this guy is a little different!* His presentations spellbound the 800 coaches in attendance and he discussed two very important aspects of his philosophy, building great movers on the court, and using eye-dominance as a key factor in training players.

Like Lluis, Pato, Toni Nadal, and Cascales too, Jofre is obsessed with developing fluid and graceful movers on the court. His approach to footwork training is somewhat progressive and modern in the sense that he likes to use shorter duration and lower reps in his footwork training—six to ten balls generally. As discussed in previous chapters, the methods of Lluis Bruguera and William Pato Alvarez emphasize longer stamina based drills, which are a more traditional Spanish approach and rhythm of training. Jofre's style, by contrast, focuses on short and quick bursts. He doesn't subscribe to the slow rhythms of typical Spanish drills. Porta is obsessed with quickness and agility, and training the eyes and reactions. He believes in challenging the nervous system and "developing the synapses," often using novel exercises with players spinning

360 degrees in between shots or closing their eyes while demonstrating technique.

Laterality, the way the brain is wired in relationship to eye dominance, is an integral part Jofre's philosophy and method. For example, Jofre believes that players who are right eye dominant will tend to see the ball better on the forehand side with a very open stance and may gravitate to that stance frequently during training. "Carlos Moya was like this," says Jofre. For Jofre, the eye-hand coordination, eye-foot coordination and left or right side of the body's physical dominance are critical factors in his Global method of development. Interestingly, Jofre connects tactics with the vision field as well. He says: "Everything is tactics. The decision we have to take in each situation is tactics. We must have better tools to better run tactics." The vision of the game, that is, the tactic, is directly proportional to the ability to perform a motor action while retaining an overview from the peripheral vision," according to Jofre.

Jofre also believes in building a strong serve and has many unique and creative exercises for developing this important shot. In Spain, the serve is often a neglected aspect of the game, so it is refreshing to see a Spanish coach take an interest in building a world-class serve. Jofre's serving approach features drills where players take running leaps, akin to a volleyball serve, or spin around different directions before serving to get more body coil or challenge the nervous system and balance of a player. He also fatigues players with sprints or agility exercises and then asks them to serve with a high heart rate. The leg drive and balance are two key areas for Jofre, and he will have players work on their explosion and landing using plyometric boxes and other devices on the court.

In addition, from my conversations with Jofre at his academy, discipline or *disciplina* in Spanish, suffering, and hard work were all clearly a recurrent theme. Jofre's stresses these values and he is a strict disciplinarian on the court. I would say he could be the toughest and strictest coach I have studied with in Spain rivaled only by Pato Alvarez or Toni Nadal. Jofre spent time in the military, and he runs a very tough boot camp style program. His coaches do not shy away from yelling at students if they are being lazy, and students are frequently "punished" in Jofre's words (although Jofre insists that actually the players are "punishing themselves;" in other words, they bring it on themselves). On my last visits to the academy, I observed many players doing lonely laps out in the hot sun in the parking lot for various infractions. Laziness is not tolerated and students are expected to be focused and engaged on the court or face punishment. It's an old school tough-love approach.

While the on-court training can be no-nonsense, strict, and intense, the off-court environment is laid back, loving, and caring. The primary force for this is Afiza, Jofre's amazingly friendly and loving wife, who is ever present at the academy, and who dotes on all the players as if they were her own. Jofre's off-court demeanor is also very friendly and caring, and he frequently flashes a beaming smile or shares a funny moment with his players. Thus the balance of toughness and love creates a uniquely critical yet supportive environment for the players.

Jofre likes to greet new students by saying, "welcome to hell," with a sardonic grin. Indeed, many students find the training too grueling and the discipline on the court too intense, and they look for alternative academies with a more chill on-court vibe. As Jofre says, if they need something like that, there are hundreds of academies in the world that can offer luxury and coddling. Never one to pamper kids, Jofre says many times parents ask him for leniency and he often responds, "They cannot buy what I am not selling!" If players do not meet his very high standard, Jofre admits that he will often "fire them." By "firing" he means he will kick them out of the program. Indeed, as a case in point, a family from New York told me that their top-ranked player was asked to leave last summer due to lack of sufficient effort (he transferred to Nadal's academy nearby).

Because players know they are at risk of being booted out, the ones who stay are compliant and motivated. By being willing to "fire" kids, which most other competitor academies will never do for fear of losing income, Jofre ensures a very special atmosphere imbued with intensity and focus, with no distractions from recreational or lazy players that could affect the group dynamic.

In many ways, Jofre is similar to Pato, Lluis, Toni Nadal, and Cascales. He creatively combines elements of the six secrets into his method and instills discipline and a strong work ethic in his players. He works tirelessly for the betterment of his students, and he demonstrates the creativity, personality and ambition of Lluis and Pato, the toughness of Toni Nadal, and the intelligence of Antonio Cascales. When not riding his motorcycle or traveling to give coaching workshops to share his knowledge, Jofre can still be found passionately working on the court developing champions on the beautiful island of Mallorca.

Chapter 11

Important Spanish Coaches and Players

This chapter will present many great players and coaches important to the history of Spanish tennis and provide a brief background on each star. The Spanish coaches and players—and the connections between them—can be hard to remember and discern. Some players here are also famous coaches too! In fact, it's remarkable how many top Spanish players stay in the game by coaching and pass their knowledge down to the next generation. This generational approach is an important part of Spain's recipe for tennis success.

By understanding the key players and coaches in Spain—like fitting together the pieces to a historical tennis puzzle—a picture can be made clearer vis-a-vis the tennis timeline, tennis lineages, and tennis alliances in the country. That representation can help the reader better understand Spanish tennis in totality and how Spain was able to dominate the tennis world. The names are listed in alphabetical order for easy reference.

Juan Aguilera was born in Barcelona in 1962 and he earned a career high ranking of No. 7 in the world in 1984. He was trained by Lluis Bruguera and famous for his consistent slice backhand!

Roberto Bautista Agut was born in 1988 in Castellón de la Plana, and he reached a career high of No. 9 in the world. He is currently coached by Tomas Carbonnell and Daniel Gimeno Traver. He was formerly coached by Pepe Vendrell, whom he started working with at the Ferrero Tennis Academy.

Carlos Alcaraz is the teenage prodigy from Murcia who catapulted to No. 1 in the world in 2022 and won the US Open in 2022 and Wimbledon in 2023, and the French Open and Wimbledon in 2024. Since his teenage years, he was guided and developed by Antonio Cascales and Juan-Carlos Ferrero and the team at Ferrero Tennis Academy in Villena. He is considered by many to be the future of Spanish tennis who may herald a new era and style of tennis in Spain.

Nicolás Almagro was also born in Murcia in 1985 and reached a career high ranking of No. 9 in the world. He was also coached for many years by an Ferrero Tennis Academy coach, Samuel Lopez. Almagro has had success coaching on the pro tour, most recently with Danielle Collins.

Julián Alonso was born in 1977 in Canet de Mar and reached a career high of No. 30 in the world. He was known for his big serve. He has had success coaching on tour and recently started working with Leylah Fernandez.

Jose Altur reached a career high No. 88 in the world and is a top coach in the Valencia region. He co-founded TennisVal Academy with Pancho Alvarino and most recently Lozano-Altur Academy. He helped develop many famous players such as Marat Safin, Dinara Safina, Igor Andreev, Taro Daniel, and other top professional players. Altur also coached David Ferrer.

Pancho Alvarino is an elite junior coach and former Fed Cup coach of Spain, who co-founded the now closed TennisVal academy with Jose Altur. Alvarino has developed numerous top junior and professional players like Dinara Safina and most recently Paola Badosa. Alvarino has a new academy project named Pancho Alvarino Academy.

José Luis Aparisi was born in 1969 in Valencia. He has coached Tommy Robredo, Pablo Andújar, Guillermo García López, David Sánchez and Cristina Torrens Valero, among others.

Pablo Andújar was born in Cuenca in 1986, and resides and trains in Valencia. He reached a career high of No. 32 in the world and was coached on tour by Marcos Esparcia. Jose Luis Aparisi also coaches Pablo during his career.

Jordi Arrese was born in Barcelona in 1964 and he earned his highest career ranking of No. 23 in 1991. Arrese was a Lluis Bruguera student known for his big topspin forehand. He also won a silver medal for Spain in the 1992 Olympics in Barcelona (narrowly losing 8-6 in the fifth set to Marc Rosset).

Paola Badosa was born in New York in 1997 and reached a career high of No. 2 in the world in 2022. She has trained in the Valencia and Barcelona regions of Spain. She has trained with legend Pancho Alvarino in Valencia at TennisVal, Xavi Budo, Javier Marti, and most recently Jorge Garcia.

Joan Balcells was born in Barcelona in 1975 and reached a career high No. 57 on the ATP Tour. Balcells was unusual because he loved to serve and volley, which is a very rare style of play in Spain. Balcells coached for many years at the Emilio Sánchez Academy in Barcelona.

Alberto Berasategui was born in Bilbao in 1973 and reached a career high of No. 7 in the world. He was coached by Javier Duarte. Berasategui was famous for his extreme western topspin forehand grip and for hitting the ball with the same side of the racquet strings. He was the runner-up to Sergi Bruguera at Roland Garros in 1994.

Galo Blanco was born in 1976 in Oviedo and reached a career high of No. 40 in the world. Gala co-founded the 4Slam Academy in Gava, near Barcelona, and he has transitioned from player to coach working with many ATP professional players such as Milos Raonic, Karen Khachanov and Dominic Thiem.

Carlos Boluda was born in 1993 in Alicante and reached a career high of No. 254. He currently coaches Nuria Parrizas Diaz on tour. Boluda trained at the Ferrero Tennis Academy for many years and was once dubbed the "new Nadal."

Joan Bosch was the coach of Carlos Moya for many years. Born in Menorca, Mallorca he has been the technical director of the Balearic Federation, worked with Jose Higueras José Perlas, and now is a senior coach at the Rafa Nadal Academy.

Sergi Bruguera was born in 1971 in Barcelona and reached a career high of No. 3 in the world and won two Roland Garros titles in 1993 and 1994. Sergi was coached by his father Lluis Bruguera. Sergi was known for his heavy topspin forehand, like Alberto Berasategui. Sergi broke the 18 year Grand Slam drought for men in Spain when he won the 1993 French Open.

Jordi Burillo was born in 1972 in Mataro, near Barcelona, and reached a career high of number 43 in the world. He is also a coach and notably worked with big serving Julian Alonso.

Pablo Carreño Busta was born in 1991 in Gijon and reached a career high ranking of No. 10 in the world. Carreño Busta trains at the Ferrero Tennis Academy in Villena and his traveling coach is Samuel Lopez. He developed as a pro under the guidance of Cesar Fabregas, Samuel Lopez, and and the whole team at Ferrero Tennis Academy including Juan Carlos, himself, and Antonio Cascales. He won the bronze medal in singles at the 2020 Tokyo Olympics, beating Novak Djokovic in the bronze medal match.

Álex Calatrava was born in 1973 in Germany and reached a career high of No. 44 in the world. Interestingly, Calatrava lived in California from 1989-91 and was coached by Spanish legend Jose Higueras. During that time, he became the top junior in California.

Tomás Carbonell was born in Barcelona in 1968, and he reached a career high of No. 40 in the world. Carbonell was a protégé of William Pato Alvarez. Carbonell was an excellent doubles player reaching a career high of No. 22 in the world. He won the 2001 French Open mixed doubles title with Virginia Ruano Pascual. He was most recently coaching Roberto Bautista Agut part-time.

Sergio Casal was born in 1962 in Barcelona and reached a career high of No. 31 in the world and No. 1 in the world in doubles with Emilio Sánchez. Sergio co-founded the Sánchez-Casal Academy (now known as the Emilio Sánchez Academy) in Barcelona. Sergio was one of Pato's "little ducks" and had a rare attacking and serve-and-volley game, which is atypical for a Spaniard.

Francisco Clavet was born in 1968 in Madrid and reached a career high ranking of No. 18 in the world. He was another one of Pato Alvarez's star students. Clavet was known as a great fighter on the court, like many other Spaniards. He is one of many tough lefty Spanish players who reached the top of the pro game. He was coached for many years by his brother and former ATP player, Jose Clavet.

Àlex Corretja was born in 1974 in Barcelona and reached a career high of No. 2 in the world. He is one of the best Catalan tennis players in history. He was the runner-up at Roland Garros twice (1998 and 2001) and won the year-end ATP Tour Championships in 1998. After his playing career, Corretja coached Andy Murray and other pros and from 2012 to 2013 he captained the Spanish Davis Cup team. Correjta also has coached at different clubs in the Barcelona area.

Albert Costa was born in Lleida in 1975 and reached a career high No. 6 in the world. He won the French Open in 2002. After his playing career he transitioned to coaching, as many former tennis players in Spain do. He was the technical director for the CIT/Catalan Tennis Federation and has worked at private clubs in Barcelona. He has also been the director of the Barcelona Open, which is hosted by the Real Club de Tenis Barcelona.

Carlos Costa was born in 1968 in Barcelona and reached a career high No. 10 in the world. He grew up playing at the Real Club de Tenis Barcelona, a prestigious private club in the north of the city. After retiring from tennis he became a sport agent, most famously managing the career of Rafael Nadal.

Nuria Párrizas Díaz was born in 1991 in Granada and reached a career high of No. 45. She lives and trains in Valencia and is coached by former professional player Carlos Boluda.

Javier Duarte is a veteran Spanish coach and former Davis Cup captain who has worked with many top players such as Alberto Berasategui.

David Ferrer was born in 1982 in Xàbia, Alicante, and reached a career high of No. 3 in the world. He was the singles runner-up at Roland Garros in 2013. He resides in Valencia and runs Academia de Tenis Ferrer with his brother Javier Ferrer. He was coached by Javier Piles for many years, Jose Altur, and Francisco Fogués. Ferrer was known for his fighting spirit and humility on tour, and he has admitted that his tennis idol growing up was Sergi Bruguera.

Juan Carlos Ferrero was born in 1980 in Ontinyent, Valencia, and reached a career high of world No. 1 in the world in 2003. He won the French Open that same year. Ferrero had an all-court game and preferred hard courts over clay—and he presaged a new Spanish mindset and style of game. Ferrero was coached since childhood by Antonio Cascales and later joined with Cascales to build the Equelite Juan Carlos Ferrero Academy (now Ferrero Tennis Academy), which has produced countless top professional players like Pablo Carreño Busta and Carlos Alcaraz. Ferrero has transitioned into coaching after his retirement and is most famous for working with Carlos Alcaraz and guiding him to the No. 1 ranking.

María Teresa Torró Flor was born in Villena in 1992, and she reached a career high number 47 on the WTA tour. Villena is a small town in Alicante where the Ferrero Tennis Academy is based.

Alejandro Davidovich Fokina was born in Malaga in 1999 and reached a career high of No. 21. His junior coach was Manolo Rubiales, and his coach on tour is Spanish coach Jorge Aguirre. He is one of only a few top Andalusian players from Spain. Most of the top players from Spain are from the Valencia, Barcelona, and Mallorca areas.

Gala León García was born in Madrid in 1973, and she reached a career high of No. 27 on the WTA Tour. She stirred some controversy when she was appointed the first female captain of the men's Davis Cup team in 2014.

Anabel Medina Garrigues was born in 1982 in Valencia and reached a career high of No. 16 on the WTA tour. Garrigues was also an excellent doubles player reaching a career high No. 3 in the world and winning the French Open in 2008 and 2009 with Virginia Ruano Pascual. Garrigues became a professional coach after retiring from singles, most notably with 2017 French Open winner Jelena Ostapenko. She was also captain of the Spanish Fed Cup team.

Angel Gimenez was born in 1955 and reached a career high of No. 42 in the world. He is a senior coach at Emilio Sánchez Academy. If you hear a coach shouting very loudly during drills at ESA, it's probably Angel!

Andres Gimeno was born in 1937 and won the 1972 French Open. He also founded a popular tennis club in Castelldefels, Barcelona, called the Club de Tenis Andres Gimeno. He was inducted into the International Tennis Hall of Fame in 2009.

Daniel Gimeno-Traver was born in 1985 in Valencia and reached a career high of No. 48 in the world. He has transitioned to pro coaching and is working with Roberto Bautista Agut.

Marc Gorriz was born in Barcelona in 1964 and was yet another tough left handed professional player on tour from Spain. He reached a high of No. 88 in the world. Gorriz, like many other Spanish professional players, transitioned into coaching after his playing career. He has worked with many top 100 players such as Alberto Martin, Albert Portas, Fernando Vicente, and Sergi Bruguera. He is currently head coach at the Rafa Nadal Academy.

Marcel Granollers was born in 1986 in Barcelona and reached a career high of No. 19 in the world in singles and No. 4 in doubles. Nearing retirement, Granollers has started an academy with Pere Riba at the Real Club de Barcelona.

Óscar Hernández was born in Barcelona in 1978 and reached a career high No. 48 in the world. He has transitioned to coaching in Barcelona and currently has a program called Master Tennis Barcelona in Sabadell in the northern Barcelona suburbs at the Tennis Club Cercle Sabadelles 1856.

Rubén Ramírez Hidalgo was born in 1978 in Alicante and reached a career high of No. 50 in the world. He lives in Alicante and has transitioned into coaching. His new venture is RC Tennis Pro Alicante and he is training players out of the Sport Club Alicante.

Jose Higueras was born in 1953 in Barcelona and reached a career high No. 6 in the world. He learned his game at the famous Real Club de Tenis Barcelona 1899 and his boyhood idol was Manolo Santana. Jose was known for his fighting spirit, sportsmanship, and humility on the pro tour. He has been living in Palm Springs, California for decades and consults with players in Palm Springs. He has also been active as a tour coach working with many American players, most famously Jim Courier and

Michael Chang. He has coached many other top players such as Roger Federer, Sergi Bruguera, and Carlos Moya. Jose also led the USTA Player Development program as director of coaching for many years working with many of the best American professional prospects.

Feliciano López was born in 1981 in Toledo and now resides in Madrid. He reached a career high ranking of No. 12 in the world in singles and No. 9 in doubles. Lopez was another top lefty Spanish player. He had a rare serve-and-volley game for a Spanish player. He won the Roland Garros doubles title in 2016.

Guillermo García López was born in 1983 in La Roda, Albacete, and he reached a career high ATP ranking of No. 23. He was coached by José Luis Aparisi and Diego Dinomo. García López is friends with Juan Carlos Ferrero and used to train at the Ferrero Tennis Academy.

Pablo Lozano was the longtime coach of top 5 WTA player Sara Errani. Lozano worked for many years at TennisVal academy and when TennisVal closed, he founded Lozano-Altur Academy with Jose Altur. Altur and Lozano are two of the top coaches in the Valencia area of Spain.

Fernando Luna was born in 1958 and reached a career high of No. 33 in the world. He was a protégé and longtime student of Lluis Bruguera and later became head coach of the Bruguera Top Team tennis academy. He's also one of the nicest guys you could ever meet!

Félix Mantilla was born in Barcelona in 1974, and he reached a career high ranking of No. 10 in the world. He was a fierce player on tour and after retiring has transitioned to coaching like so many other professional players from Spain. He has coached Alexandr Dolgopolov, Lucas Pouille, and recently Roberto Bautlsta Agut.

Javier Marti was born in Madrid and reached a career high ATP ranking of No. 170. He was once labeled the "next Nadal," along with Carlos Boluda, but never achieved high level success on tour. He has transitioned to coaching and recently worked with Paola Badosa.

Alberto Martín was born in Barcelona in 1978 and reached a career high of No. 34 in the world. He won the 1996 Junior Roland Garros title.

Conchita Martínez was born in 1972 and reached career high of No. 2 in the world. She is famous for being the first Spaniard female to win Wimbledon in 1994 and was inducted into the International Tennis Hall of Fame. Martinez is also coaching on tour and has worked with Garbine Muguruza.

Pedro Martínez was born in 1997 in Valencia and reached a career high of No. 40 in the world. He has been coached by Daniel Gimeno Traver and by Gerard Granollers, the brother of Marcel Granollers.

Albert Montañés was born in 1980 in Tarragona and reached a career high ranking of No. 22 in the world. He resides in Barcelona and has the dubious distinction of holding the record for most first-round exits (35) for Grand Slam events.

Carlos Moyá was born in 1976 in Palma, Mallorca, and was the first Spanish player to reach the ATP No. 1 ranking in 1999. He was the runner-up at the Australian Open in 1997 and won Roland Garros in 1998. He went on to coach Rafael Nadal and became a lead coach at the Rafa Nadal Academy.

Garbiñe Muguruza was born in 1993 in Venezuela and emigrated to Spain to live and train at the Bruguera Academy under the supervision of Lluis Bruguera and his team. She won Roland Garros in 2017, Wimbledon in 2018, and became world No. 1 on the WTA computer.

Jaume Munar was born in 1997 in Mallorca and has reached a career high ranking of No. 52 in the world. He is yet another professional tennis player to come from the small island of Mallorca. At 14 he went to train with the Spanish Federation in Barcelona and reached the junior Roland Garros finals in 2014. After returning home to Mallorca, he has made the Rafa Nadal Academy his training home, working with Tomeu Salva and Pedro Clar. Toni Nadal also oversees his development.

Rafael Nadal was born in 1986 in Manacor, Mallorca, and he is the greatest champion Spain has ever had. He has won an incredible 22 majors including 14 at Roland Garros. He was coached for many years by his uncle Toni Nadal and Francis Roig. He is now coached by Carlos Moya, another former player from Mallorca who reached No. 1 in the world himself as a player.

Carla Suárez Navarro reached a career high No. 6 in the world and was born in 1988 in Las Palmas de Gran Canaria (Canary Islands). Suárez is not the first professional women's player from Las Palmas. Magui Serna peaked at No. 19 in the world in 2004, and Marta Marrero was a top 50 WTA pro, and both were from Las Palmas. Suárez Navarro moved to Barcelona to receive more professional training. She was coached by Xavier Budo on tour.

Manuel Orantes was born in 1949 in Granada and reached a career high of No. 2 in the world in 1973. He is another great left-handed champion from Spain. He won the 1975 U.S. Open defeating Jimmy Connors in the final after saving five match points and coming back from 0-5 in the fourth set against

Guillermo Vilas in the semifinals. Orantes was inducted into the International Tennis Hall of Fame in 2012.

Virginia Ruano Pascual was born in Madrid in 1973 and reached a career high of No. 28 in singles and No. 1 in doubles. She was a top doubles player and won the French Open in 2008 and 2009 with Annabel Medina Garrigues and many more major titles with her partner Paola Suarez. She also won the French Open mixed doubles with Tomás Carbonell in 2001.

Jose Perlas is an elite Spanish coach who worked with Carlos Moya when he won the 1998 French Open and Albert Costa when he won the 2002 French Open. In addition, he captained the Spanish team to win the Davis Cup twice in 2000 and 2004. He has coached many other top pros including Nicholas Almagro and Juan Carlos Ferrero.

Javier Piles was the longtime coach of David Ferrer. He is known as a tough taskmaster who believes in developing the strongest player possible physically. He has worked with many other pros like Roberto Bautista Agut and Milos Raonic.

Albert Portas was born in 1973 in Barcelona and reached a career high of No. 19 in the world. After his playing career he turned to coaching and worked with many pros like Pablo Andujar and Daniela Hantuchova. With German Puentes he runs the Portas-Puentes Ad-In Tennis Academy in Barcelona at the prestigious Club Tennis Barcino.

Tommy Robredo was born in 1982 in Hostalric, Girona, and reached a career high of No. 5 in the world. He was coached by Jose Clavet, Francisco Clavet's brother, who also coached Àlex Corretja, Fernando Verdasco, and Feliciano López.

Francisco Roig is a former professional player with a career high singles ranking of No. 60 and No. 23 in doubles.

He has been the second coach and travel coach for Rafa Nadal for many years. He co-founded BTT academy in Barcelona with Francis Roig and Alvaro Margets.

Tomeu Salva was born in Mallorca in 1986 and reached a career high No. 288 on the ATP tour. He is a pro coach at Rafa Nadal Academy and has worked with Jaume Munar.

David Sánchez was born in 1978 in Zamora, and he reached a career high of No. 41 in the world. He has coached after his playing career and most recently has been working with Fernando Verdasco.

Emilio Sánchez was born in 1965 in Madrid and reached a career high of No. 7 in the world in singles and No. 1 in doubles with partner Sergio Casal. Emilio was one of Pato's star students. He won the French and U.S. Open in doubles in 1988 and the French Open for the second time in 1990. Emilio is the oldest sibling in one of the most successful tennis families ever. He captained the Spanish Davis Cup team to the championship in 2008 and transitioned successfully into business and coaching after his playing career. He is the owner of the Emilio Sánchez Academy.

Javier Sánchez was born in 1968 in Pamplona and reached a career high of No. 23 in the world in singles and No. 9 in doubles. He won the junior US Open title in singles and doubles in 1986. Javier was one of Pato's protégés along with his older brother Emilio.

Manuel (Manolo) Santana was born in Madrid in 1938 and was one of Spain's greatest players for many years. He won at Roland Garros twice in 1961 and 1964, the US Championships in 1965 and Wimbledon in 1966. His achievements helped inspire Ferdinand Franco to develop and promote tennis all across Spain. He was inducted into the International Tennis Hall of Fame in 1984.

Sara Sorribes Tormo was born in 1996 in Castellón de la Plana (Valencia) and resides and trains in the same area. She reached a career high of No. 32 in the world. She is being coached by Sílvia Soler Espinosa, another former professional Spanish player.

Fernando Vicente was born in Benicarló, Castelló in 1977, and he reached a career high of No. 29 in the world rankings. Vicente co-founded the 4Slam Tennis Academy in Barcelona and has transitioned to pro coaching on the ATP Tour. He has been working with Andrey Rublev since 2015 and guided Rublev to as high as No. 5 in the world rankings. Vicente was named 2020 ATP coach of the year for his success with Rublev.

Albert Ramos Viñolas is a tough left-handed grinder who was born in 1988 in Barcelona and reached a career high of No. 17 in the world. He lives and trains in Mataro just outside of Barcelona. Ramos Viñolas has a big topspin lefty forehand and is a typical Spanish fighter from the baseline.

Gabriel Urpi was the coach of Flavia Pennetta for several years, until her retirement. He was previously the coach of Arantxa Sánchez Vicario in 1994 and 1995, during which time she won two Grand Slam tournaments and also coached Conchita Martínez to the 1998 Australian Open final. In 2017, he worked as a coach of Elina Svitolina, having also formerly coached Nicolas Mahut. In 2021, Urpí began coaching Caroline Garcia. He is a senior coach at Rafa Nadal Academy.

Fernando Verdasco was born in Madrid in 1983 and reached a career high of No. 7 in the world in singles and No. 8 in doubles. He is another excellent left-handed Spanish professional. He was coached by Diego Dinomo, David Sánchez, and Quino Muñoz.

Arantxa Sánchez Vicario was born in 1971 in Barcelona and achieved the word No. 1 ranking in singles and doubles. She is the famous little sister of Javier and Emilio Sánchez. Sánchez Vicario won 14 major titles in singles and doubles. She was coached by Gabriel Urpi during her playing career.

Jordi Vilaró is the former Davis Cup coach of Spain and captained the team during its first success at winning the title in 2000. He was the longtime coach of top 10 player Felix Mantilla and has coached many other professionals from Spain. He is cofounder and lead coach at BTT academy in Barcelona.

Juan Albert Viloca was born in Barcelona in 1973. He was a protégé of William Pato Alvarez and reached a career high of No. 47 in the world.

Nuria Llagostera Vives was born in Mallorca in 1980 and reached a career high of No. 35 in the world. She lives in Barcelona and is another great doubles player from Spain, reaching a career high of No. 5 in the world.

CHAPTER 12

Leading Spanish Academies

For anyone considering sending a player to Spain for training, this chapter is for you. Finding a suitable Spanish academy that matches what you are looking for can be a challenge due to the cultural and language differences, and the sheer distance of Spain from the United States and other countries outside of Europe. For Europeans and others from nearby countries, Spain is the most popular training ground for serious tennis. Players migrate south in a similar way that American players visit or move to Florida to train—from Russia, Eastern Europe, England, France, Belgium, Germany, etc. Sometimes I call Spain the Florida of Europe. Players and federations love to use Spain as their training base. For example, Barcelona Total

Tennis (BTT) has a relationship with the USTA, and USTA Player Development sends top American squads there. The LTA and Tennis Australia have a training base for their elite squads in Spain. Many of all the top federations around the world have a training relationship with Spain because they recognize that their players can learn a lot by training the Spanish way.

Here are profiles of some of the leading academies in Spain. One caveat: Spain's tennis academy scene has become more and more commercialized and mercenary in the past decade. Watch out for imposters—academies and clubs that are advertising themselves as world-class training destinations but do not offer elite level Spanish training. The academies listed here are top quality with a proven track record.

Every effort has been made to make the information here as correct as possible, but please check the academy's website or email the academy representative to get the most up to date current information. Many parents also reach out to me directly for advice on where to train in Spain and how to find the right fit. I am happy to help guide any reader—free of charge!

For cost analysis, please use the following rubric:

Barato—Cheap
No pasa nada—Average price
Caro—Expensive
Ay caramba!—Most expensive

Barcelona Total Tennis

www.Bttacademy.com

Location: Valldoreix, near Sant Cugat, a swanky suburban town located about 25 minutes north of Barcelona and 30 plus minutes from the Barcelona International Airport.

Facilities: 16 clay, 2 hard, pool, restaurant, gym, soccer pitch, supervised apartment housing (with free van service to the courts), hotels nearby.

Services: Psychologist on staff, physio and massage, medical arrangement with a Spanish Davis Cup sport medicine doctor. Private lessons are discouraged but they will make specific coaches available upon request.

Description/Philosophy: BTT is based at the Club Esportiu de Valldoreix, north of Barcelona, in the town of Valldoreix. The club is situated in quiet, well-kept suburban neighborhood. Lots of greenery and a quiet and tranquil location make this academy a very pleasant place to train or visit. The club has 16 clay and two hard courts, although BTT tends to use only the bottom 6-10 clay and two hard courts as the club is shared with membership. Club Esportiu de Valldoreix has an air of privilege associated with private tennis clubs but is not snobby. The club is clean and well maintained, and the courts and facilities are in good condition. The club has a small, Ferrero Tennis Academy on the premises.

BTT prides itself on its small size and the personal attention it gives to its players. The annual full-time program typically accepts only 20-25 players and BTT is actively looking for high level ITF and professional players who want to train for the professional tour. Part-timers of all levels are also welcome at BTT and receive the same personal attention as their regular annual students—which is sometimes not the case at other Spanish academies. The enrollment swells in July, the busiest time of the year, but this is still smaller than giant programs like Rafa Nadal Academy, comparatively speaking. Even in the summer, the team keeps a 2:1 coach to student ratio, which is exceptional. The coaching staff is headed by Jordi Vilaró, former Davis Cup coach for Spain, and Francisco Roig, former Davis Cup assistant coach and travel coach of Rafa Nadal. They have an international staff of coaches, including former top 10 player Juan Aguilera, who is also available for lessons or group work.

With only one to two kids per coach and court, BTT offers the most personal attention of any elite academy in Spain, perhaps rivaled only by 4Slam. You are basically getting a private or semi-private lesson in a group setting throughout most of the day. Nobody can fall through the cracks with this kind of ratio and nobody is waiting in lines. As BTT's motto says, "One player, one project." Training sessions take place daily, morning and afternoon, Monday to Friday, combining technical and tactical training with physical preparation. If there is no competition during the weekend, players have a double workout morning session on Saturday and a Sunday rest. If you are lucky, you may catch ATP player Joao Sousa training there.

Best Match For: Serious ITF or national level players are only accepted for the annual full-time program. Lower level and younger players are accepted on both a part-time basis, especially in summer, but this academy caters to high performance players looking for ultra-personal training at 1:1 or 1:2 coach to player ratios. Focus tends to be on teenage boys with fewer girls participating.

Cost: *Caro*

Emilio Sánchez Academy (ESA)

www.EmilioSánchezacademy.com

Location: El Prat de Llobregat (Barcelona), suburb of Barcelona, 15 minutes from the city center and five minutes from the Barcelona International Airport.

Facilities: 27 courts [clay, green set (hard), synthetic grass], pool, restaurant, modern gym, supervised housing onsite, hotel within walking distance.

Services: Psychologist on staff, physiotherapy and massage, sports medicine available, private lessons available with all coaches on staff.

Description/Philosophy: Formerly the largest and most commercial academy in Spain, ESA is not quite as full as in the past—and it actually seems better for this reason. The programs are more personal and smaller scale now than at the massive Rafa Nadal Academy, which has supplanted ESA as the largest academy in the country. The academy has by far the most convenient location, just five minutes from the Barcelona International Airport, which makes it a popular stop for traveling ATP/WTA players and anyone desiring convenience. The club is owned by Emilio Sánchez, not leased, and it is shared with membership, which can make for a busy, crowded atmosphere at times, especially in summer. The club is situated directly off a main highway in a commercial and agricultural area, and the dirt access road to the club could be made more pretty. Once entering the club, however, the grounds inside the gates are immaculately well kept, clean, beautiful—and very safe and secure. Don't let the entrance's lack of charm discourage you. Behind the walls of the club the training system and facilities of the academy are top-notch. The facilities of the club have many modern updates including a new dorm/educational building and a beautiful gym with modern equipment. Some visitors are turned off by alternative housing in small bungalows at the back of the club's grounds, but the trailers are clean and well-kept, and primarily used for part-time/summer campers. The bungalows were also recently renovated and upgraded to improve visitor comfort.

The academy is open to all ages and levels, and even has an adult program. Beginners to ATP/WTA players—and everyone in between—are welcome at ESA. William "Pato" Alvarez, a truly monumental and legendary figure in Spanish tennis, is sadly no longer teaching at the academy, but his philosophy and method live on. The teaching system is a real gem, well-designed and unique, and all the coaches on staff are expected to follow the system uniformly to encourage consistency of teaching quality. The system is classically Spanish, based on the philosophy of Pato Alvarez and his famous student Emilio Sánchez. There are many drills from the basket, and a highly structured practice, with players hitting a lot of groundstrokes and working on defensive positioning, as well as body positioning, footwork, and balance. The academy is also proud to work regularly on the midcourt and volley game including playing a lot of doubles (The original owners Sergio Casal and Emilio Sánchez were the No. 1 doubles team in the world).

The system of the program is generally two kids per court with five kids training on three courts and one coach supervising. For example, two players working cross court shots, two players playing points, and one player drilling with the coach, and then a rotation. However, as is common at many Spanish academies, be cautious during busy times like July when the academy numbers can swell and the ratio can be higher. Emilio is most proud of the educational system offered at ESA. Parents often say that the quality of the private school integrated onsite is a major reason for choosing the academy.

Emilio Sánchez Academy's system is similar to other Spanish academies offering 3-4 hours of tennis and 1-2 hours of physical training daily. For part-time summer players, however, the fitness sometimes is not very serious or challenging because many of the students are recreational players. This trend is common now at many academies in Spain in the summer.

Annual full-time students are usually much higher level and their training is very intense. To quote former owner and head coach Sergio Casal, "Here you have to be a fighter."

The academy also includes an excellent and professional high school, middle school, and even a new elementary school. Emilio Sánchez believes strongly in the importance of education, even for players destined to become pros. Overall, this is a friendly place where all levels of players should be able to get good quality Spanish training. Just be careful that your player does not get lost in the crowd, especially during busy times. The academy offers a special program that features a daily private lesson, which is the best package available. The coaching team is professional, organized, and well-trained, and head coach Stefan Ortega is caring, talented, funny, and charismatic.

Best Match For: All players at all ages and levels, from beginner to professional who would like to be immersed in the original Spanish method of drills based on the philosophy and method of the legendary Pato Alvarez.

Cost: *Caro*

Bardou Tennis Academy

www.Bardoutennisacademy.com

Location: UP Sports Club in Cornellà, a suburb of Barcelona just 10-15 minutes from the city center and 15 minutes from the international airport.

Facilities: 31 courts (clay and hard, 1 indoor court), gym and heated indoor pool, lockers and physiotherapy, pro shop.

Services: Psychologist available, physiotherapist and massage services available, stringing, private lessons are available.

Description/Philosophy: This facility in the heart of Cornellà has been purchased by an investor group which includes former Spanish professional player Tomas Carbonell, and it is undergoing many upgrades and renovations. Sadly, the 4 indoor tennis courts are now only one. Three courts were converted to padel courts! The UP Club is convenient to the city center and the airport. The expansive complex of clay and hard courts is not in the most scenic area and is bounded by a highway and roads in a commercial district. It is currently leased out to many different individual coaches and private academies, not just Bardou. The grocery and shops of Cornellà are, however, walkable from the club.

The method and philosophy are based on the approach of Lluis Bruguera, a true legend in Spain, who still participates in the program and advises the coaches. Lluis also works on the court, especially with the high competition players. Head coach Ricard Ros is one of the friendliest and caring individuals a parent could ever want to work with their kids. This academy is the Bruguera tennis academy, reconstituted since its closing during the pandemic. The academy still offers the friendly vibe and serious training that Bruguera Top Team was famous for.

Best Match For: All levels of players from young juniors to elite national and ITF players to touring pros who are looking for legitimate Spanish training based on the method and philosophy of the legendary Spanish coach Lluis Bruguera—all at a reasonable cost.

Cost: *No pasa nada*

Academia de Tenis Ferrer (ATF)

www.Academiatenisferrer.com

Location: La Nucia, about 45 minutes from the Alicante airport and 1.5 hours from the Valencia Airport.

Facilities: 9 courts (6 clay and 3 hard, all lighted), pro shop, gym, hotel and residences near the facility, restaurant, swimming pool, soccer fields, athletics track.

Services: Psychologist available, physiotherapist and massage services available, medical services, stringing.

Description/Philosophy: Javier Ferrer started ATF around 2010 at the Jávea Tennis Club and now the academy has a brand new facility built in partnership with the city of La Nucía. The academy is a short 15 minute drive from the beaches of Benidorm. The headquarters of the academy is now located in La Nucia next to the Ciudad Deportiva Camilo Cano, although the team still manages the original club in Jávea, which is now focused more on recreational training, adults, and a small pro group.

Javier Ferrer leads a very professional team at both clubs and is the leader and director of the academy. David Ferrer, the famous tennis champion and former pro player from Spain, provides star power and advises on training methods and philosophy. The method and philosophy are based on Javier's experience as a coach and the key pillars that brought success to David Ferrer during his professional career. Javier has an adaptable approach based on player individuality. The training is intense and focuses on consistency, good movement and defense, and racquet speed/weapon development, among other areas. The values that David Ferrer demonstrated in his career are taught such as humility, hard work, sportsmanship, education, perseverance, and social commitment. Javier Ferrer says, "We create elite players, but we also create people."

The academy is smaller in size and features an excellent 2-3 player per court and coach ratio. ATF has a new collaboration with Elian's British School of La Nucia to offer an excellent private education to its players.

Best Match For: Serious players from young juniors to elite national and ITF players to touring pros. Adults can receive high-quality training at the Javea facility.

Cost: *No pasa nada*

Global Tennis Team

www.globaltennisteam.com

Location: Marratxi, Mallorca, close to Palma.

Facilities: 5 clay courts, small dorms and lounge area, restaurant, gym.

Services: Physiotherapy, massage, and psychologist services available. Private lessons with Jofre or his staff are available. Sports medicine services are available.

Description/Philosophy: Global Tennis Academy is where leading Spanish coach, Jofre Porta trains future professional prospects. It is in a pleasant, quiet, and secluded area, about 20 minutes from Palma de Mallorca International Airport and the city of Palma. Jofre, a charismatic coach who developed the first ever Spanish No. 1 player in the world, Carlos Moya, and also helped guide Rafa Nadal in his formative years, calls his small school, "A dollhouse... where we do not want to be slaves to growth."

Players can expect small groups and personal attention. On a recent visit, two boys from Italy (17 and 15), one girl from London (14) and a coach from Slovenia about 23 years old who was accompanying two of his players had nothing but really positive things to say. They were all in awe of Jofre's coaching skills. Jofre is there in the morning and the afternoon sessions and often overlooks all five courts from his balcony—shouting at players and coaches from above. The kids can also take privates from Porta or his staff. The academy has many top-ranked national Spanish juniors in its stable. Global says that there are a lot of Russian students who train year-round there, as well as native Spanish players. The format is often different than at some other academies. A common practice structure is that players are mixed and all do the same thing as the others regardless of level. A typical session might include spending 20 minutes per court and then rotating to the next court. One court, for example, might focus on "consistency," another defensive shots or attack shots, or tactical work.

The academy is strict and tough. Some players find it too tough. Jofre often will "fire" kids he doesn't feel are working hard enough. He will kick them out. The coaches are authoritarian and some parents have complained about this aspect. In the end, Jofre wants tough, hard-working kids in his program and no weak links. Marshmallow kids will not survive here; at Global they build soldiers.

Best Match For: Serious players who are single-minded enough to train hard in a remote location with no frills.

Cost: *No pasa nada*

PRO-AB

www.proabtennis.com

Location: Central Barcelona, 10-15 minutes from the Barcelona International Airport and close to the city center.

Facilities: 7 clay courts, pool, no supervised housing (but can house with local families), gyms nearby, restaurant/cafe, hotel nearby, local schooling option (most players are local Spanish players from Barcelona).

Services: Psychologist available, physiotherapy, massage, stringing, and sports medicine available.

Description/Philosophy: PRO-AB is in the Barcelona city in a relatively urban area. It is based at Club Espiritu Hispano Francés, an aging but serviceable sports club in a middle-class neighborhood in the city. The club boasts a lovely pool area and an aging clubhouse. The courts are in good condition and PRO-AB has use of seven of the 11 red clay courts for its training and use of hard courts nearby. They have access to two gyms including an advanced techno-gym 10 minutes from the club. Carla Suarez Navarro is one example of a top Spanish player who has trained under the guidance of Josep Arenas and his well trained staff. Josep is an experienced Spanish coach who trains mainly local Spanish players in the area who are looking to progress up the ITF circuit, but he also accepts international visitors. The training is authentically Spanish, but Josep insists that he is more technical than most other Spanish teachers. PRO-AB has about 20 full-time players in its competition school and they are looking for mainly ITF and professional players to join the school full-time. The key to PRO-AB's success and system, according to Arenas, is the small family atmosphere where everyone is known personally and no player slips through the cracks. This is no commercial factory with assembly line training—just good authentic Spanish style training on the red dirt. Players train about 3 to 3.5 hours of tennis and 1.5 hours minimum physical per day, which is a typical schedule in Spain at many academies.

Best Match For: Serious, high-level ITF and nationally-ranked players who want an authentic Spanish training experience in a small, intimate program with no frills. Spanish language skills are helpful!

Cost: *No pasa nada*

Lozano-Altur Academy

www.Lozanoalturtennisacademy.com

Location: Situated in the outskirts of Valencia, about 20 minutes from the Valencia International Airport.

Facilities: 12 clay and 2 hard courts, gym, restaurant, boarding offsite, hotels nearby, stringing, privates are available.

Services: Psychologist available, physiotherapy, massage, sports medicine services available, privates are available, school options locally and online.

Description/Philosophy: Nestled into some Valencian orange fields, Lozano-Altur is based at a private club where the program leases 12 clay and two hard courts and shares the club's facilities with the membership. The club and the courts are in good condition but some of the structures are aging. This is another no-frills style academy, like the former

Bruguera academy and PRO-AB, where you don't come for the fancy equipment, you come to train hard the Spanish way under the tutelage of experienced professional coaches. In this respect, you are in very good hands because the owners and head coaches of Lozano-Altur are Jose Altur, former top 100 player and now top high performance coach, and Pablo Lozano, superstar coach. Jose tends to specialize in the boys' training and Lozano tends to work with the girls.

Best Match For: Serious tournament level juniors and aspiring pros who want a no-frills academy, small numbers, and who want to train under the watchful eyes of Lozano and Altur.

Cost: *No pasa nada*

Ferrero Tennis Academy

www.ferreroacademy.com

Location: Near the town of Villena. Closest major city and airport is Alicante (30 minutes) or Valencia, which is an hour plus drive away.

Facilities: 10 clay courts and 7 hard, 1 indoor court, 1 stadium hard court, 1 synthetic grass court, Playsight equipped courts, gym, 2 pools, restaurant, supervised dorms onsite, hotel bungalows onsite, 400m track, soccer field.

Services: Psychology, medical and physio, and massage services all available, schooling (private online options), private lessons available.

Description/Philosophy: Built around Juan Carlos Ferrero's private estate is this beautiful, modern facility where only serious players need apply for the annual program. The catch is that you have to drive more than one hour from the nearest international airport in Valencia to get to the academy, which is built literally in the middle of farmland, basically in the middle of nowhere. Roll up to the private gated entrance with the letters JC on the front, and when the gates open, prepare to be dazzled by a modern and impressive training facility right next to Juan Carlos Ferrero's private house!

The academy is definitely focused on developing top pros and has a tremendous track record, led by Antonio Cascales and Juan Carlos Ferrero. Cascales is a legendary coach in Spain and Juan Carlos is the former No. 1 player in the world and now coach to Carlos Alcaraz. An experienced team leads the ITF and ATP groups. Carlos Alcaraz and Pablo Carreno-Busta both train at the academy frequently, which is really inspiring for the junior players who are there. The summer camp, however, tends to be more recreationally focused and there is definitely a separation between the summer players and the annual ones. On a recent visit in the summer, one parent expressed frustration that her highly ranked son enrolled for the summer was not allowed to join the annual training group of players. If you have $2,000 handy, you can get an hour private lesson with Juan Carlos Ferrero himself!

Best Match For: Serious tournament juniors and aspiring pros who want to be around ATP stars and trained by one of the best coaching teams in the world. Players must be hyper-focused and able to train in a remote location with a strict code of conduct without going stir crazy.

Cost: *No pasa nada*

4Slam

www.4slamtennis.com

Location: Gava Mar, Barcelona area

Facilities: 9 courts (5 clay, 4 hard), swimming pool, apartments and hotel options nearby.

Services: Physiotherapy, nutrition, medical services, medical services, massage, stringing.

Description/Philosophy: 4Slam has one of the best locations of any Spanish academy, just 10 minutes from the Barcelona International airport and 15-20 minutes from the city center. The academy is tucked away in a modest residential and commercial area of Gava, on a nondescript dirt road, a short drive from the beach. Behind the entrance gate is a small but modern and elite professional training center. People just passing by would never know that some of the best players in the world of tennis have been recently developed there, such as Milos Raonic, Karen Khachanov and Andrey Rublev.

4Slam was founded by former ATP pros Galo Blanco, Fernando Vicente, and Jairo Velasco. Vicente currently travels with Rublev on the ATP Tour. The founders strongly believe in a professional approach, with a focus on personal attention, low student to coach ratio, hard work, humility, and willingness to suffer. The coaching team is very professional and experienced, and the players work hard in a typical Spanish program with very serious fitness. A typical day features about 3 hours of tennis and 2.5 hours of fitness daily. The academy has an online school collaboration with Laurel Springs and AESA Prep International.

Best Match For: Serious competitive juniors focusing on ITF results and aspiring professional players.

Cost: *Caro*

Rafa Nadal Academy

www.Rafanadalacademy.com

Location: Manacor, on the eastern part of the island of Mallorca

Facilities: 37 (and growing) courts at the academy (19 hard including a stadium court, 3 permanent indoor courts, 7 semi-indoor clay courts, 8 outdoor clay courts, and 7 additional clay and one indoor court at the Rafa Nadal Club adjacent to the academy (the academy shares these courts with the local community). Synthetic turf fields, various residence options onsite including a modern hotel, multiple Ferrero Tennis Academys, sports museum, pro shop, restaurants, sports bar, pools (indoor and out) and spa, and school facilities onsite, even a Crossfit gym!

Services: Psychologist on staff, physio and massage, sports medicine available, private lessons available with all coaches on staff, and anything else you could possibly want!

Description/Philosophy: While Manacor, home to the academy, is not as pretty as the beach town nearby called Porto Cristo, where Rafa now lives, it serves as a huge magnet for elite tennis players in Spain and around the world, and many lower level players too. The Rafa Nadal Academy is not very easy to get to: multiple flights are generally involved to get to Palma International Airport and then about a 45 minute ride to get to Manacor and the academy. Some people love the place and believe it's worth the trip; some people don't. The academy could be described as the Disneyland of tennis academies in Spain—an unforgettable experience for some visitors, especially those who idolize Rafa himself.

The massive RNA campus is fresh and modern looking—perhaps borderline antiseptic and clinical with its steel and mortar edifices—and everything is newly built. The academy continues to evolve and grow, building out new facilities—such as their beautiful new semi-indoor red clay courts—and developing star players like Felix Auger-Aliassime and Casper Ruud, just to name a few. That star power is special and Rafa himself can still be found practicing at the academy when he's not traveling. While Toni Nadal was supervising the academy in the early years, he has since taken a more active role traveling and coaching on tour, most recently traveling with Felix Auger-Aliassime. Nevertheless, Toni's method and philosophy still permeate the academy.

The academy is large and draws many different kinds of tennis players to Manacor: recreational adults and juniors, serious tournament players, ITF, and professional players. RNA's creation and powerful presence in Spain has had a huge influence on the tennis academy scene in the country. The academy has pulled many players who would have gone to train in Barcelona, Valencia, or Alicante to Mallorca instead, and RNA has forced many other academies to adjust their business models and training methods to compete better. The word earth-shattering comes to mind. Nevertheless, RNA has a lot of competition from mainland competitors and even from others on the island itself.

The academy services are not cheap. At last check, a week of camp or academy can run higher than 2,000 euros per week—the most expensive prices in Spain. The facilities, however, are top-notch and very sophisticated. The coaching can be great, especially if you have an elite player who gets attention from the top coaches like Carlos Moya, Marc Gorriz, Gabriel Urpi, Tomeu Salva and Joan Bosh.

Some parents have reported that lower level kids can get lost in the mix—especially in the summer—and that the coaching and fitness can be uneven in quality at times. Those are common concerns at other large academies around the world, too. Some parents have also expressed concerns about the communication from the reception and the organization at RNA. The academy manages a lot of kids and hosts many tournaments, so if there is rain, for example, scheduling and organizing the practice day can be hectic.

The character building program and values promoted by Toni Nadal are the real gem of this academy. Toni is a genius coach and believes in building humble champions who will be good citizens of the world. The academy has a broad array of services including professional psychology, sport science, nutrition, and other programs to support the RNA athletes. The academy also features an evolving professionally managed school onsite.

RNA is very safe and secure, almost feeling locked down like a fortress at times. Players are supervised very carefully. During the week players typically don't do excursions as they are busy with training and Manacor is not great for walking to activities from the academy. On the weekends the staff is very good about supervising excursion trips to the beach or other charming towns like Porto Cristo or Port de Soller, or the city of Palma, Mallorca is an incredibly beautiful place-like a paradise—especially around the coastal beach areas of the island.

Annual players tend to have 2-3 players per court but summer and short-term players can expect up to 4 players per court. Summer can be a busy time with enrollment swelling and many recreational players visiting the academy.

Best Match For: Players of all ages and levels who are diehard Rafa fans and want to visit his hometown, experience the museum, and train in the system of Toni Nadal surrounded by ATP stars like Rafa, Felix Auger-Aliassime, and Casper Ruud. Also a good option for very high level ITF and ATP pros who can gain access to the high level coaches at the academy. The academy is expensive but offers exceptional facilities and luxury.

Cost: *Ay Caramba!*

SotoTennis Academy

www.Sototennis.com

Location: Sotogrande, Andalusia region.
Facilities: 6 courts (3 clay and 3 hard), gym, and many offsite housing options.
Services: Psychologist available, physiotherapy, nutrition, massage, sports medicine services available, stringing. School options locally and online.
Description/Philosophy: Soto Tennis, based out of El Octogono Club in Sotogrande, is a small family academy and the creation of former British No. 1 in doubles Dan Kiernan. The

club is well situated in a pretty area just minutes away from the beach and Sotogrande Marina. Sotogrande is near the southernmost tip of Spain, not far from the rock of Gibraltar. Interestingly, the area was originally developed as a gated community and designed to be "the Palm Springs of southern Europe." The academy, the most southern Spanish program featured in this book, is a one hour drive from Malaga airport and about 25 minutes from Gibraltar airport. Players have a choice of several different accommodations such as independent living in nearby apartments by the marina, host families for younger kids, and hotel options, and many are walkable to the club. Be aware that one parent reported that the academy does not offer supervision during the middle of the day for day campers. The club is situated very close to the beach and marina, which makes for a special venue indeed. The prices of training at Soto Tennis are lower than the rates in the Valencia or Barcelona areas—very reasonable indeed.

The academy has improved over the years and features a strong physical training and tennis team, led by Kiernan. Kiernan is a big believer in sport science and uses experts in strength and conditioning, psychology, nutrition, and physiotherapy in a team approach to help his players. Sport science is an important pillar in the method at Soto.

The academy draws players from all over the world but particularly from Kiernan's home country of Britain. Players produced by the academy have had particular success in doubles at the ITF and pro level. Recently the academy has hosted training blocks for ATP and WTA players like Dan Evans, Iga Swiatek, and Tamara Zidansek, among others. Soto has a particular focus on graduating players to the American college tennis system.

Best Match For: Serious players of all ages and levels who desire a personal, family run program. Soto is a good option for budget conscious families as well.

Cost: *Barato*

I sincerely hope that this chapter will help parents, coaches, and players find the best academy in Spain that fits their needs. The academies are ever-evolving so please be sure to check online for the latest information, as some material here may grow out of date. If you have further questions about individual academy strengths and weaknesses, please feel free to email me directly at chris@chrislewit.com. I love to talk about Spanish tennis! I have many parents and coaches who contact me for help finding the right academy fit in Spain, and I'm always happy to share my knowledge. It is rewarding to receive emails from parents telling me that their son or daughter had a positive tennis and cultural experience in Spain at one of its world-class academies. Finding the right academy fit for the player's personality and needs is the most important priority.

Chapter 13

Nadal, Alcaraz, and the Secrets

The incredible rise of Spanish tennis to lead the world has been propelled to new heights by one man in particular: Rafael Nadal. Arguably the greatest player of all time with 22 major singles titles to his name and a truly incredible 14 Roland Garros titles, Nadal epitomizes the Spanish values of hard work, willingness to suffer, and humility. In addition, Nadal's tennis game beautifully demonstrates the key pillars that I argue are the secrets of Spanish tennis. Nadal has incredible movement and balance. Nadal has a massive forehand weapon and high racquet speed. Rafa is very consistent and frugal when it comes to giving unforced errors. His defense is legendary. He is one of the fittest players on tour. And Rafa can endure and suffer like no other champion. Nadal is the paragon of all the Spanish virtues discussed in this book!

Despite Nadal's achievements, in the last decade or so Spanish tennis was in a rut. Legendary Spanish coach and former professional player Angel Gimenez says, "Spanish tennis was down for a while, but now things are getting better." One of the reasons there is a lot of hope and excitement in Spain is because of the potential of Carlos Alcaraz. The young Alcaraz has won two major singles titles, at the U.S. Open in 2022 and Wimbledon in 2023, but many in Spain believe that he will fill the void after the Nadal era. Nadal himself has recognized and publicly acknowledged that Alcaraz has passion and spirit that reminds Rafa of himself. Although their games are different— Alcaraz is a more aggressive all-court player than Nadal—they both have star power and star talent. Alcaraz, with his infectious smile and charming charisma, could be the next big star for tennis. If he can start winning more major titles, he will help drive more participation and interest in tennis in Spain.

Nadal's story is well documented. He was trained by his Uncle Toni Nadal starting at a young age. Toni pushed him hard. He was a demanding coach, "exigent" as Toni likes to say. Toni taught Nadal from a young age all of the core elements found in this book, especially the footwork aspect, forehand weapon, consistency, defense, and fighting spirit. Interestingly, Toni says his one regret was that he did not do enough professional fitness and injury prevention work with the young Rafa. Rafa basically just played tennis and soccer as a kid, says Toni. Soccer was his cross-training.

Nadal's movement skills are legendary. In his movement you can see efficiency, "economy" as the Spanish super coach Jose Higueras likes to say. Nadal's "support system" is very strong, which means he sets up for shots with a good wide base of support from which to load his energy and send it into the ball. His balance is preeminent and he reads the court exceptionally well. Uncle Toni did a great job developing Rafa's eyes and feet using some of the exercises mentioned in Chapter 1.

One of Toni's obsessions is the forehand and the footwork to get inverted on the forehand. Toni has stated, "the forehand is the most important shot in the professional game." He really prioritized developing that weapon in Rafa's arsenal, and he concurrently relentlessly trained Rafa's inverted footwork movement since he was a kid. Even today, the run-around forehand—*the drive invertido*—is probably Rafa's best shot. Toni Nadal insists that working on inverted shots not only trains the shot itself, but really helps developmentally to improve the reading and measuring in the eyes, the subtle inverted footwork steps, and the balance of the athlete because most players don't feel as comfortable moving around the ball in the inverted way. Toni likes to put the player in this uncomfortable inverted situation and develop the eyes, feet and balance this way.

In terms of Rafa's forehand weapon, the racquet speed and the RPMs are incredible. Rafa's spin rate has been measured to be one of the highest on tour. When Rafa was a kid, Toni loved to do some of the quick feeding drills explained in this book to help develop Rafa's hand and racquet speed.

Alcaraz, like Rafa, also demonstrates mastery of the secrets of Spanish tennis described in this book. Alcaraz is an example of a modern Spanish built player with clean, conservative grips and technique who can take the ball early to attack the net but also defends well deep into the backcourt. He moves exceptionally well, like Rafa Nadal, and Alcaraz has been trained as a kid using many of the movement drills outlined in Chapter 1.

Carlos has a tremendous forehand weapon, similar to Nadal. He can generate huge power but can also step back and grind with good topspin and RPM. Unlike Nadal, on the forehand side, Alcaraz has a conservative grip, almost eastern, which his coaching team at Ferrero Tennis Academy confirmed in a personal interview. Antonio Cascales, who oversees Alcaraz's training along with Juan Carlos Ferrero, revealed that Alcaraz's grip is so conservative that he can drop shot off the forehand side without changing the grip. This advantage makes his drop shot essentially unreadable. Carlos can rip the ball for big power on the forehand, spin it, or drop shot the ball with perfect disguise, which makes his forehand a very special weapon indeed.

Alcaraz is a very consistent player. He has done all the work and exercises explained in Chapter 3: the wall, many hand fed consistency drills, and the classic Spanish live ball consistency drills. Alcaraz is very comfortable on red clay and can grind when he wants. Although sometimes Alcaraz is erratic with his decision making, and he can get too impulsive and aggressive, he has put in the work to be consistent when he needs to. Many young kids looking up to Alcaraz just admire his sexy drop shots or explosive forehand winners. Says Jordi Vilaro, former Davis Cup coach of Spain, "Alcaraz in some ways makes our job tougher in Spain as coaches. All the kids want to copy what he does but not everyone has the talent to do what he does. Kids do not realize that Alcaraz has put in the hard work over the years to develop an incredible base of consistency. He can tap that well of consistency any time he needs to grind and be solid at important junctures of a match.

Alcaraz is already almost a legend for his defense. He scrambles well and can get to almost any ball. He counterpunches and defends as well as Nadal, and moves just as quickly to save himself when being attacked. Alcaraz demonstrates the classic Spanish ability to both attack and defend very well. His skills on defense give him a good chance to win major titles and other prestigious events on slow red clay, while his offensive capabilities promise great success on fast surfaces.

Alcaraz is very comfortable on multiple surfaces and grew up playing on both red clay and hard courts. There is a growing trend in Spain to develop all-around players who can win on any surface. In the 1980s and 1990s, many Spanish players were clay court specialists. That mentality and philosophy has changed all over Spain. Today, Spanish academies have installed more hard courts and coaches stress taking the ball earlier and attacking on fast courts in combination with the great defense Spanish players have always been known for. This evolution is reminiscent of a similar evolution during the same time period in the sport of professional mixed martial arts. In the 1990s, there were many successful pro fighters who just grappled and had great Brazilian Jiu-Jitsu skills. That's no longer the case. Those types of specialists are not the norm in pro MMA anymore. Rather, similar to what has happened with Spanish tennis players, modern MMA fighters have retained their great defense and grappling skills from BJJ and added more stand up attacking/striking skills. Modern fighters have a balance of defense and offense and are versatile and multidimensional in their games, very similar to modern Spanish tennis players.

Alcaraz's fitness is very high—almost legendary—and on par with Rafa Nadal's endurance. Alcaraz seemingly never tires as exemplified in the 2022 U.S. Open where he won three back-to-back, five-set matches and was physically superior to his rivals. Alcaraz became the third player to reach a major final having won three consecutive five-set matches, after Stefan Edberg at the 1992 U.S. Open and Andre Agassi at the 2005 U.S. Open. At 23 hours and 39 minutes of play duration across his seven matches, Alcaraz spent the longest time on court in major history.

Alcaraz is built thick and strong with broad and he is curiously developing biceps reminiscent of Nadal's. Carlos has ripped legs, moves extremely fast, and also has tremendous flexibility around the court. He could be the fastest athlete and best mover on the pro tour in today's game, according to many analysts. I would love to see him and Rafa in a footrace! Alcaraz's speed allows him to recover from disadvantageous situations, defend the court, and counterpunch spectacularly.

Alcaraz's capacity to suffer is another key to his success. Like Nadal, he fights until the end and enjoys the battle. Alcaraz's fighting spirit and willingness to suffer are important components of his success and a big key in the secrets of Spanish tennis.

It is of course tempting to compare Alcaraz with the egendary Nadal in terms of skills and ability, but one must not forget that Nadal is arguably the greatest player ever and that nobody in Spain can compare with his heavyweight record. As Lluis Bruguera keenly observes, to compare Alcaraz with Nadal, who owns 22 major singles titles, "is almost an insult to

Nadal." Nevertheless, even Nadal himself sees some similarities to Alcaraz in their mindset, passion for the game, and fighting spirit.

Said Nadal, "He (Alcaraz) doesn't have to look at me anymore. He's a star already. He's doing amazing things. Happy [for] a Spanish colleague, happy about being a fan of the sport that we're going to have an amazing player for such a long time." Nadal has also said that he thinks Carlos has a great team around him to guide him and that there should be many more major titles in his future.

Juan Carlos Ferrero, former No. 1 player in the world from Spain and coach to Carlos told the ATP staff, "He [Alcaraz] is a ferocious competitor. He competes to the end of every match." In addition Juan Carlos added, "I've enjoyed how he plays since he started with me. I know that he will have those moments of genius. I always give him free rein to be creative, not a robot. Those things come naturally to him."

"We call it Hot Shot," Ferrero told Sportskeeda, and he admitted that they practice these shots regularly. "We often rehearse those kinds of shots in training in case they come up. We joke about appearing on Tennis TV as the Hot Shot of the week. They are natural shots that he comes up with, but you have to have skill."

Ferrero told Sportskeeda about Alcaraz's game and personality: "He has a special way of connecting with people, it's really magnetic," said Ferrero. "The way he gives his all on court and plays, with that intensity and speed in his shots. He can do so many things during a match and that's what people are entertained by. I enjoy watching him play, and I've been involved in the world of tennis for so long."

Emilio Sánchez, former Spanish top 10 player and owner of Emilio Sánchez Academy is extremely laudatory of Alcaraz: "He has come as a lightning bolt, a shot to the heart, a blessing to our sport, not just because of how he plays but because of who he is, because of his humility, because of how much he arrives at people's hearts. That's why I am in front of my computer, writing down the similarities to the greatest of all times. He's a simple guy who really loves tennis and the audience feels it, people get excited, they even jump off the bench. Carlos plays and wins, he does everything, I can hardly remember any player at his age with so much tennis. I have been around tennis for many years, seeing stages of young athletes become great, but this time, Carlos can be called one of the most exceptional young tennis athletes."

Astute observers like Emilio Sánchez compare Alcaraz to an amalgam of the Big 4 – Roger Federer, Novak Djokovic, Rafael Nadal, and Andy Murray. Says Sánchez: "I would say that he has the technique like Federer, the tactics like Murray, the physical side like Djoko, and the mind like Rafa."

Says Sánchez, "(Alcaraz) is reminiscent of Federer in terms of the range of technical options and how he uses the slice backhand to handle the exchange. The movements are more like Nadal." Sánchez continues, "At 19 years old, he already possesses Djokovic's flexibility and great balance that allows him to defend without losing court position, and he is able to change his game with fluency." Sánchez adds, "Tactically he has the skill to read the game, this is a quality that brings him closer to Andy Murray, a master at finding the opponent's weaknesses." Regarding his mind, Sánchez says, "Alcaraz's mental ability, the ability to think like a champion reminds me of Rafa's. He is able to forget mistakes and give his best no matter the situation."

Spanish tennis was down in terms of top 100 players for a decade or so in the early 2010s and many were concerned that Spain might disappear from the top of the game when Nadal finally retired. Those thoughts have shifted with the rise of Alcaraz.

Since the publishing of *The Secrets of Spanish Tennis* in 2014, Spanish tennis has been able to survive and prosper. Most notably is the continued success of arguably the GOAT, greatest of all time, Rafael Nadal, and the meteoric rise of Carlos Alcaraz, who has captivated the tennis public's imagination. Nadal has managed to solidify his place in tennis history and—almost simultaneously—Alcaraz has reached No. 1 in the world and won four Grand slam titles.

Emilio Sánchez has always talked about the importance of generations in Spain—older players helping the next wave—as discussed earlier in this book. Here is another very good example of that with Alcaraz, who was inspired as a kid by Nadal, and mentored as a teenager by the Spanish former world No. 1 Juan Carlos Ferrero.

Alcaraz certainly seems like the real deal, but the reader should know about the cautionary tale of Carlos Boluda, from Alicante, who was similarly touted as the next great Spanish champion, "the next Nadal," and who also trained at the Ferrero Tennis Academy. Boluda struggled on the pro tour and only reached a career high of No. 254. Alcaraz has far surpassed that achievement already and has reached No. 1, but there is no guarantee that he might not stumble somehow. In addition, watch for the possible rise of Martin Landaluce, the 2022 junior U.S. Open champion, for example, and countless other young stars inspired by Rafa and now Alcaraz. Could players in Spain ask for better role models?

Juan Carlos Ferrero says that what makes Alcaraz special is not just his talent as an athlete, but his character: namely, that he is humble, works hard, listens respectfully to what he is told and always believes in himself and never gives up. Indeed, Alcaraz displays tremendous "docility"—the quality that Antonio Cascales believes is so important for a player to have.

Both Nadal and Alcaraz are products of a training methodology that prioritizes the six secrets of Spanish tennis, as described in this book. As Rafa's career comes to a close, it remains to be seen whether Alcaraz can carry the mantle for Spain or whether a new Spanish star will shine. Regardless of what country dominates world tennis, the training system from Spain will continue to thrive and evolve, helping both native-born Spanish players and others around the world learn the secrets that produced so many champion players in the last decades.

CONCLUSION

The future of Spanish tennis looks relatively bright. While the years of having fifteen or more ATP players in the top 100 may not be achievable again, Spain consistently has between six and ten, which is comparable to other top nations. The entire country is waiting on tenterhooks to see if Alcaraz can be the next great champion for Spain for many years to come, filling the enormous shoes of Rafael Nadal. Paula Badosa has climbed to as high as No. 2 in the women's rankings, which is a very positive sign on the WTA side as well.

A relatively unknown story is how many current world-class players who play for foreign nations have been trained in Spain or influenced and guided by Spanish coaches. That number is quite significant and reveals the great impact Spain still has on the professional tour—a huge ripple effect felt around the global tennis community—even as it seems clear that the success of the 1990s and 2000s may not be matched again by native Spanish born players.

Therefore the story of Spain's tennis dominance is in a state of flux. There is a transformation underway from the remarkable achievements of Spanish greats like Nadal, Moya, and Ferrero and solid performances by countless journeyman professionals. Spain is becoming more well-known as a world-class *entrenador*, or trainer, with continued solid performances by its players but with a more prominent role in developing and influencing the best players in the world, many of whom happen to not be native-born Spaniards.

The tennis scene in Spain is also in transition as Spanish academies proliferate and the country becomes more well known as a destination for high level tennis training and coaching matched perhaps only by Florida in the United States. No other destination offers such myriad high level training and coaching options. There are world-class academies like ESA, Bardou, BTT, Pro-AB, and 4Slam, just in Barcelona alone, with elite training centers like Global Tennis, Ferrero Tennis Academy, Lozano-Altur, Rafa Nadal and others scattered across the rest of the country. There are also many *splinter academies*—smaller programs where top coaches have left the more well-known academies to go independent. The splinter academy phenomenon is something new in Spain and makes navigating the academy landscape even more difficult for foreigners. Unfortunately, some of these smaller, independent academies can be trusted but others are clearly mercenary— perhaps predatory even—trying to take advantage of the reputation of Spanish tennis, and they do not offer high-quality training. Overall, however, Spain has metamorphosed from a scrappy, underdog tennis hopeful to a world-leading coaching powerhouse with some of the best high-performance training options—in just a matter of decades. Truly remarkable.

In addition to the native-born players in the top 100, here is a short sample of premier players who have trained in Spain or have been or currently are guided by Spanish coaches:

Qinwen Zheng (Pere Riba)

Milos Raonic (Carlos Moya and Galo Blanco)

Alexander Dolgopolov (Felix Mantilla)

Grigor Dimitrov (ESA)

Andy Murray (ESA and Pato Alvarez)

Fabio Fognini (Jose Perlas)

Karen Khachanov (Galo Blanco and Fernando Vicente —4Slam)

Andrey Rublev (Galo Blanco and Fernando Vicente—4Slam)

Santiago Giraldo (Alex Corretja)

Richard Gasquet (Sergi Bruguera)

Taro Daniel (Jose Altur)

Nicolas Mahut (Gabriel Urpi)

Dusan Lajovic (Jose Perlas)

Frances Tiafoe (Jose Higueras)

Joao Sousa (BTT and Francis Roig)

Tomas Berdych (Dani Vallverdu—who is ESA trained)

Thus, in the future Spain may no longer lead the world in native-born players, but the Spanish influence on the global stage is still quite profound. The country is open for business—the tennis academy business—and ready to train juniors and pros from other countries. In addition, Spanish methods are becoming more understood and practiced by coaches around the world who are trying to raise their own standards and results. Furthermore, a diaspora of excellent Spanish coaches and former world-class players are available for hire on the junior and pro circuits—and they are in high demand.

This "Spanish Effect" has been felt in the United States perhaps greater than anywhere else in the world. By sheer serendipity, one of the Spanish greats, Jose Higueras, came to live in the United States in Palm Springs and got involved with the USTA and American players. In the early years, he started working with American players like Michael Chang, Jim Courier and Todd Martin, with great success. More recently, Higueras has transformed the USTA coaching system and culture, bringing many Spanish drills, methods, and philosophies to USTA national and regional coaches. That effort has led to many top American talents having direct access to Jose's Spanish wisdom and indirectly to many Spanish approaches and principles as implemented by the USTA team. The results have been phenomenal with American tennis growing leaps and bounds, especially on the WTA side. The current group of men are very successful with more players in the ATP top 100 than Spain! The American story is a great specific example of how the Spanish coaching diaspora has made the global tour more competitive for Spain itself. The same effect is happening all across the world as national systems adapt and compete in a global game: It's survival of the fittest.

While legends like Nadal will eventually retire and there are high hopes for Alcaraz to make new history, the Spanish legacy and recognition will live on through the education and development of players from around the world who are not all native-born Spaniards, but play "Spanish" nonetheless. These players are the *New Spanish Armada*.

Emilio Sanchez recently published an incisive article about the future of Spanish tennis on his blog and he alludes to important subjects and themes in this book. Emilio says that the extensive club system (built by Franco) needs to carry the load of producing competitive players again. Emilio also remarkably admits that he is guilty, along with many other academies, of selling Spanish tennis methods more to foreigners than native-born players. He calls on Spanish coaches and academies to re-engage with native born players again with the support of the Spanish Federation (RFET) to help put Spain back on top of the tennis world. His article is included here as a special section:

The Rise of American Tennis and the Future of Spanish Tennis—Emilio Sanchez's Call To Action

In 2016 I wrote an article comparing Spanish and American tennis. Upon moving to Florida in 2012 I observed the changes made by the USTA (United States Tennis Association) to its calendar and found them to be accurate. Considering this data, I anticipated that it was only a matter of time before many American players would ascend to the ATP rankings top 100 as it had happened in the 1990s and early 2000s. My analysis was strongly criticized by some sources in Spain and even by some players and coaches, who thought I was wrong in saying that the United States would overtake Spain even though it had led in player production for the last 40 years.

At the time of that review, Spain had had 15 players in the top 100 that year, 11 at the time of the article, but 7 of them were over 30 years old. However, there were several factors that were changing. Spain had almost no young players in the top 500, while the USA already had 10. If the data were analyzed from bottom to top, the question arose as to how the best generation of tennis players that Spanish tennis has produced, led by Rafa Nadal, David Ferrer, Feliciano Lopez, Fernando Verdasco, Roberto Bautista, Pablo Carreño, Albert Ramos, Carlos Moya and Juan Carlos Ferrero, etc. would be replaced.

COUNTRY RANKING

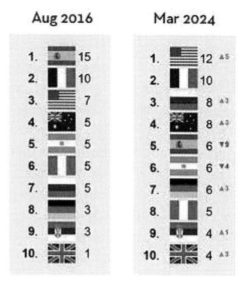

Aug 2016   Mar 2024

Eight years have passed, and the numbers speak for themselves. Spain has gone from 15 players to only 6 in the top 100, placing it in the fifth position, while the United States has increased from 6 to 12 players, placing it at number one. Virtually all the Spaniards who were at the top are now retired and we have not been able to replace them. The most worrying data is found at the base of the pyramid, where if we analyze the ages and number of players, we find that Spain has gone from having about 140 players with ranking in 2005 to 90 today, compared to the United States which has increased from 120 to 210. This remarkable increase brings countless opportunities for Americans in the next 10 years.

Although recently Spain has been fortunate to have Alejandro Davidovich in the top 20 and to experience the explosion of Carlitos Alcaraz, who with the majesty of his game has generated illusion and hidden our shortcomings, the publication of the ranking last week with only 6 players in the top 100 evidence this new reality more clearly. The Royal Spanish Tennis Federation (RFET), with Miguel Diaz at the helm, began to change its strategy three years ago and created the pyramid of Spanish tennis tournaments, following the system implemented by the United States more than a decade ago, moving from Futures tournaments to Challengers. To do so, he multiplied the aids and increased the number of tournaments. However, this work may take 5 to 7 years to bear fruit and for Spain to return to having more opportunities as in its golden age, it will also be necessary to bring players up from the junior stages and to have more competitive groups that want to make the transition to professionalism. We must fill that bottom of the pyramid if we want to go back on top.

This arduous and laborious effort does not give results from one day to the next. We must increase the level and then create or take positions, and we have some super talents that will move up, such as Martín Landaluce or Daniel Rincón. However, even if they succeed, if they are not accompanied on the journey by between 140 or 150 players in the middle part of the ranking (between positions 100 to 2000), these gifted players will be very lonely.

I would like to encourage the network of Spanish clubs to keep pushing, to become part of the tennis pyramid by training in their clubs, competing and above all improving the level to make the competition grow, even if it is hard. Spain does not have unlimited funds from a major tournament as the USA does, but it has the clubs that the Anglo-Saxon country lacks. For the most part, these clubs are the engine that drives players and creates professional tennis players, and this is where we must continue to make a difference, by managing to place more young people in the transition from youth to professional level. And I can't help but to be self-critical as a club and as an academy, since many of the competition schools of these clubs have become social and the competition groups no longer travel as they used to. In parallel, the academies and best coaches dedicate our main resources to foreigners, who are the ones who pay the bills. At this point, we should all together with the federation be an active part of the pyramid, participate by betting on some Spanish players and encouraging renowned coaches who have managed to teach the Spanish model to so many champions to be part of this pyramid that we sell so much.

If we look at the list of players coached by Spaniards in their development we find Djokovic, Rublev, Zverev, Khachanov, Lajovic, Zheng, Sakkari, Ruud, de Minaur, Fils... the list is endless. What if we dedicated only half or less of that quality of Spanish coaches to Spanish players, where would we be? Here the federation should be the point of union and collaborate with many of those best coaches in the world to get them involved and everything would change in a short time. Still, it is a big cultural change because the federation has not worked with private coaches. To give an example, in my academy for 25 years and after producing more than 20 top 100 foreign players ourselves, we have never been approached by the federation to help them with any Spanish players. I know for a fact that most of those top coaches have never been approached either.

My last question is, if for 40 years Spain produced more than 100 players in the top 100, where are they now? How is it possible that some of them are not involved in the pyramid? Fortunately, many of them are the driving force behind the clubs and academies. For me, the same change that has started with the tournaments must be done with the coaches who are known to be valuable, to implement that culture of the tennis player, and that return to enjoying the transition from junior to professional.

In my years of traveling and studying in Spain, the hard work and dynamism of Lluis and Pato and the six core training keys—the secrets included in this book—became, for me, the best way to understand Spanish tennis success. Those secrets will live on, whether in Spain itself, or around the world through the diaspora of Spanish coaches and the proliferation of Spanish philosophy and methods. I sincerely hope that the reader has enjoyed this survey of Spanish tennis, its training methods, history, about the country's leading tennis coaching figures and players, and its top academies. I wrote this book because I believe in the power and efficacy of the Spanish way and that coaches, parents and any student of this great game who has never been to Spain or learned the Spanish "system" can really benefit by being exposed to the core philosophies and methods in this book. In many ways, there was a perfect storm that contributed to Spain's incredible rise to world dominance in the last decades. I hope this book captures and conveys the essence of that success. It remains to be seen whether Spain and its training methods and philosophies will stand the test of time.

Already, one can see the beginning of an evolution in the coaching and training paradigms. Hard courts are now commonplace and more and more coaches are emphasizing aggressive tennis with less defensive movement. Indeed, Alcaraz may be the paragon and harbinger of this more aggressive Spanish style. If the spotlight stays on Alcaraz, he will surely dramatically influence the way the game is played and taught in Spain. I'm sure the system will also evolve even further as the next generation of coaches add their collective expertise and stand on the shoulders of Pato, Luis and the other Spanish legends. How will Spain's methods evolve over the next decades and will they be able to remain a world tennis superpower? Will Spain develop new secrets? Only time will tell the answers. For now, I hope you enjoyed learning the contemporary secrets of Spanish tennis. Good luck using these methods on your own— and don't forget to practice suffering amigos!

Helpful References

Chris Lewit YouTube Channel—daily uploads about Spanish tennis and junior development

SecretsofSpanishTennis.com—the official book website with free videos of every drill

ProdigyMaker.com—The official Chris Lewit blog with many articles and quotes on Spanish tennis

The Spanish Federation—www.rfet.es

The leading private Spanish teaching organization—www.rptenis.org

USTA Player Development— www.usta.com/About-USTA/Player-Development

The USTA Player Development website offers resources on the Spanish style because Spanish coach Jose Higueras, former head of coaching, redesigned the national training curriculum with many Spanish influences

The USPTA—www.uspta.org—offers many videos and other resources on the Spanish style of training as taught by Emilio Sánchez and Luis Mediero, followers of the
Pato Alvarez method

ICI—icitennis.org—The International Coaches Institute, led by Luis Mediero, is an organization that trains coaches in the Spanish method

The Prodigy Maker Show and The Secrets of Spanish Tennis podcast--great resources on Spanish tennis training methods and philosophies

"Spanish Tennis Coaches and Drills Facebook Group—best resource for latest Spanish tennis news and training methods

Spanish Tennis Lingo

Here is a cheat sheet of Spanish tennis vernacular that is frequently encountered on the court. These are local sayings that I have learned over the years from Spanish coaches. Many students are confused when they first start training in Spain because of the tennis colloquialisms the coaches use. If a player is training in Catalonia (Barcelona or Mallorca for example), the situation is even more confusing because coaches will often intermingle Spanish terms with Catalan words, which is doubly confusing. This list of sayings will help you or your player bridge the language barrier. *Buena suerte*! Good Luck!

La derecha —The forehand

The drive—Also the forehand

L'esquierda—The backhand

The reverse—Also the backhand

Drive invertido—Run-around forehand

Sigue—Continue. Keep going

Eso es!—That's it! Great!

Camina—The literal translation is "to walk' but often means *sigue*, or keep moving, keep going

Accompany the ball—Possibly Toni Nadal's favorite saying. The same as "the line"—the extension of the racquet along the pathway of the ball, helping to bring control and depth to the shot

The line—A term frequently used by Lluis Bruguera meaning the extension of the racquet along the pathway of the ball, helping to bring control and depth to the shot

Support system—A term made popular by Jose Higueras meaning the wide foundation of the legs for the shot and using the legs during each swing

Plataforma—The platform. The support system. The legs and stance

Las Piernas—The legs. Spanish coaches are obsessed with players using the legs more and more and more

Los Pies—The feet. Spanish coaches are obsessed with players using their feet to measure well the distance between their bodies and the ball

Los ojos—The eyes. Spanish coaches are obsessed with the reading of the court and the pathway of the incoming ball

Los manos—The hands. Spanish coaches want a fast hand or hands because the coaches are obsessed with racquet speed.

Ahora!—Now!

Change speeds—A commonly heard term in the Bruguera method describing the acceleration of the racquet on its pathway to impact with the ball. The racquet should be slow during the backswing and then fast as it meets the ball

Change levels—Bruguera lingo meaning low-to-high pathway of the racquet to lift the ball up through the impact point and to help impart topspin

Mas alta—Higher. Basically the coach will say this if the player is not hitting with enough margin over the net

Bien—Good

Buena—Good

Muy bien—Very good!

Excellente—Excellent

Exacta—Exactly

Para—Stop in Catalan

Abierto/a—Open or wide shot or serve

Angulado—Angled. Angled sharply to open the court

Efecto—Spin on the ball, especially topspin, which is an obsession in Spain

Corta—Short as in hitting a shot short in the court

Defensa—Defense

Attaque—Attack

Dejada—Drop shot

Contradejada—Counter drop shot

Potencia—Power

Velocidad—Velocity

Aceleración—Acceleration

Saque—Serve

Saque con efecto—Serve with spin

La ret—The net

Jugador—Player

Entrenador—Trainer or coach

Fisica/Fisico—Fitness is the most important part of the Spanish training day

Gymnasio—The gym. The most important place in the Spanish tennis academy

Fútbol—Soccer, the favorite hobby and second favorite sport of Spanish tennis players

Disciplina—Discipline

Psicologia—Psychology

Respeto—Respect

Sufrir—To Suffer. The most important aspect of character for Spanish players

Cubo—A bucket, often used traditionally to hold balls in Spain

Pelota—Ball

Raqueta—Racquet

Pista—Court

Cancha—Court